Legal Machines

JCL Studies in Comparative Law: Second Series

Series Editors

Professor William E. Butler

Professor Michael Palmer

1. W. E. Butler and O. V. Kresin (eds.), *Discovering the Unexpected: Comparative Legal Studies in Eastern and Central Europe* (Clark, New Jersey, Talbot Publishing, 2021). ISBN 9781616196554

2. Simon Palmer and Zhai Xiaobo (eds.), *Bentham Around the World* (Clark, New Jersey, Talbot Publishing, 2021). ISBN 9781616196561

3. O. V. Kresin, *Comparative Law in Warsaw: 1800-1835*, transl. W. E. Butler (Clark, New Jersey, Talbot Publishing, 2022) ISBN 9781616196585.

4. W. E. Buler and O. V. Kresin (eds.) *The Comparative Method in the Science of Law* by Lev Rebet (Clark, New Jersey, Talbot Publishing, 2022) ISBN 9781616196653

5. Horst Dippel, *Modern Constitutionalism*, 2 vols. (Clark, New Jersey, Talbot Publishing, 2022) ISBN 9781616196769

6. Stephan Meder, *Legal Machines*, Clark, New Jersey, Talbot Publishing 2023) ISBN 9781616196813

STUDIES IN COMPARATIVE LAW
SECOND SERIES

Legal Machines

OF SUBSUMPTION AUTOMATA, ARTIFICIAL INTELLIGENCE, AND THE SEARCH FOR THE "CORRECT" JUDGMENT

Stephan Meder
PROFESSOR FOR CIVIL LAW AND HISTORY OF LAW
GOTTFRIED WILHELM LEIBNIZ UNIVERSITÄT HANNOVER

TRANSLATED FROM GERMAN BY
Verena Beck

TALBOT
PUBLISHING
Clark, New Jersey

ISBN: 978-1-61619-681-3

TALBOT PUBLISHING

AN IMPRINT OF
The Lawbook Exchange, Ltd.
33 Terminal Avenue
Clark, New Jersey 07066-1321

Please see our website for a selection of our other publications and fine facsimile reprints of classic works of legal history www.lawbookexchange.com

Library of Congress Cataloging-in-Publication Data

Names: Meder, Stephan, 1956- author. | Beck, Verena, translator.
Title: Legal machines : of subsumption automata, artificial intelligence, and the search for the "correct" judgment / Stephan Meder, Professor for Civil Law and History of Law, Gottfried Wilhelm Leibniz Universität Hannover ; translated from German by Verena Beck.
Other titles: Rechtsmaschinen. English
Description: Clark, New Jersey : Talbot Publishing, an Imprint of The Lawbook Exchange, Ltd., [2023] | Series: JCL studies in comparative law, second series ; no. 6 | Includes bibliographical references and index. | Summary: "Examines the metaphor of the legal machine and discusses current questions of legal technology and legal decisions by algorithms"-- Provided by publisher.
Identifiers: LCCN 2022058895 | ISBN 9781616196813 (hardcover)
Subjects: LCSH: Law--Decision making--Data processing. | Artificial intelligence--Social aspects.
Classification: LCC K212 .M424 2023 | DDC 340/.1--dc23/eng/20230105
LC record available at https://lccn.loc.gov/2022058895

Printed in the United States of America on acid-free paper

Table of Contents

Preface

Machine metaphors have long been of interest to jurisprudence. The German historian and constitutional jurist August Ludwig von Schlözer (1735-1809) stated, towards the end of the eighteenth century, that "the most instructive way" to teach constitutional law was to treat "the State as an artificial, exceedingly composite machine". Jurists involved in finding legal decisions would therefore be merely a cog in an enormous apparatus whose function is to give expression to the will of the sovereign through law-abiding application of the law. The nineteenth century declared war not only on the absolute monarchical State but also on the mechanistic paradigm. The critique of a "mechanical" application of law and the distorted image of the "subsumption automaton" have stood for criticism of judging that, far removed from the demands of "everyday life", adheres to predefined concepts and makes reflections on law and justice utterly dispensable. Rudolf Jhering's "judgment machine", Hermann Kantorowicz's "thinking machine", or Max Weber's "paragraph automaton" can be seen as pejorative images of machines into which "one throws the files at the top, together with costs and fees, so that it spits out the judgment at the bottom, along with the more or less valid reasons". All these machines are caricatures of the legal method that prohibits the judge from reaching independent decisions even when the circumstances of the individual case call for it.

A clear distinction must be drawn between these older machines and the self-teaching legal machines equipped with artificial intelligence that are currently being discussed as autonomous technical systems, legal tech, or subsumption automaton 2.0. Here too, of course, these machines do not come out of nowhere, but rather go back a good fifty years. The first computer-based concepts for formalizing decision-making rationality opened a field of research for Contemporary Legal History that has hardly been explored, not least because of the astonishing diversity of its interdisciplinary, methodological, and legal-theoretical approaches. The devices, automata, machines, and systems presented herein may vary greatly in their details. However, they share in common that decisions made with their help risk failing to recognize the individuality of cases and the special features that give a particular event its distinctiveness. This observation goes beyond jurisprudence and leads to the fundamental question: what differentiates the achievements of human thought processes from the decisions and judgments made by machines and artificial intelligence?

Regarding the translation into English, I have received strong support from many quarters. First, I would like to thank Verena Beck for her translation of a text that was as complex as it was challenging. My thanks also go to Stefanie Reuß for her competent editing of the manuscript and for compiling a comprehensive bibliography, which is not available in the German edition. In addition, I would like to thank Gregory Talbot for his support in the publishing of the text. Last but not least, I would like to thank the co-editor of this series, Academician William E. Butler, for his valuable comments and suggestions as well as for his thorough review of the manuscript.

Hanover, November 2022

Introduction

"Digitization" is pervasive in politics, the economy, education -- and also in jurisprudence. Learning algorithms and autonomous systems are assuming functions traditionally reserved for humans. We speak of "artificial intelligence" when activities that require consideration or decision-making are left to machines. Ten years ago, a book asked provocatively whether we were seeing "The End of Lawyers".[1] What role will new technologies play in public prosecutors' offices and in courts? Could legal robots be making suggestions for verdicts and sentences? How long before they are able to make decisions independently? Or will they merely be used to review standard cases, to process recurring legal questions that require an increased computing effort? Do standard cases even exist? Is not every case different? Do not all the circumstances in each individual case require consideration?

Phrases such as "*judex non calculat*" (judges do not calculate) or "*error calculi non nocet*" (a calculation error does no harm) have stood the test of time for millennia. Calculation errors do not become legally binding in a judgement according to German law (§ 319 ZPO) and can be corrected at any time. How much longer will this be so? Must the lines between calculating, considering, and deciding be redrawn? And what will happen if the machine makes a mistake? Is the robot liable for damages? Can it attain consciousness and should it then be accorded legal capacity? Must the entire legal order then be reexamined? These are some of the questions which the move towards digitization in the social order will bring to the law. The unstoppable process is made possible by increasingly powerful computers, a process that

[1] R. E. Susskind, *The End of Lawyers? Rethinking the Nature of Legal Services* (rev. ed.; 2010). When questions of legal judgments and legal thinking are raised herein, they are to be understood in a broad sense. They encompass not only the rulings of judges, of the administration, or of professors who discuss judgments or solve hypothetical cases. They include private adjudication or governance, as well as the opinions of lawyers or the decisions they set out in their briefs. Given the particular openness of legal thinking (see chapter 8), the ultimate issue is the differences between human and artificial decision-making in general.

penetrates to the core of all legal activity, to that last enigma that the term "application of the law" cannot adequately encompass.

Learning algorithms are in a position to draw logical conclusions and verify the validity of arguments. Has our perception of the "application of law" been changed by digitization without us noticing? What does "application of law" actually mean? And why is the term so contentious? Could these new technologies determine the application of the law to the point where it will no longer be humans but machines that decide?

These questions are not new: "*Lex ex machina*" is a vision of which humankind has dreamed for some time. The ideas of the rule of law, impartiality, the binding postulate, and hopes for rationalization and simplification of the law meant that the judicial "judgement machine", the celebrated "subsumption automaton", appeared to be the ultimate goal. To date such machines merely symbolize the jurist; they are a metaphor for the ideal bureaucrat who can resolve any conceivable legal case by means of deduction and subsumption according to purely logical and mechanical principles.

AUTOMATA IN THE FIRST LEGAL MACHINES AGE

This ideal originates in at least the seventeenth century – the first legal machine age which commenced approximately a century before the Industrial Revolution. Influenced by the first French theorist of the State, Jean Bodin (1529-1596), a political philosophy centered around such concepts as the social contract, sovereignty, war, and the machine began to dominate. One co-founder of this theory was the mathematician and legal philosopher Thomas Hobbes (1588-1679), who famously described the natural state as a state of war. Because humans are by nature wolves vis-à-vis other humans, he argued, the situation required the conclusion of a social contract, the purpose of which was to end the state of nature by transitioning into a state of law. The consensual transfer of undivided power to a *single* sovereign was intended to secure peace and protect private property. Even though such a contract was never actually concluded,

Hobbes believed that it signified a pivotal moment and the proper beginning of history. He explicitly qualified the social contract as an act of creation (*imitatio creationis*) which created an "artificial man", the artifact of a machine that could make the state appear in the form of an automaton. In his state-philosophical treatise of 1651, Hobbes named the automaton "Leviathan".[2]

Other authors expanded upon the machine metaphor. The French scientist and philosopher René Descartes (1596-1650) is worthy of mention, as his rationalism conceives the unity of the world as a mechanism -- a gigantic clockwork machine switched on by a sovereign will and powered by it reliably and constantly.[3] Anybody making a legal determination would be a tiny cog in an enormous machine whose function consists of giving voice to the sovereign will of the ruler.

Immanuel Kant (1724-1804) resorted to the image of a machine. It soon became clear to him that an entity such as the State eludes direct observation and can only be imagined "symbolically" as a concept of reason. In an oft-cited passage, he summed up the connection between enlightened absolutism and the machine:

> Thus, a monarchical state is represented by a living body, if it is governed by national laws, and by a mere machine (like a hand-mill) if governed by an individual absolute will; but in both cases only *symbolically*. For between a despotic state and a hand-mill there is, to be sure, no similarity; but there

[2] Thomas Hobbes, *Leviathan: Or the Matter, Forme and Power of a Commonwealth Ecclesiastical and Civil*, ed. Michael Joseph Oakeshott (1957); German edition: *Leviathan oder Stoff, Form und Gewalt eines bürgerlichen und kirchlichen Staates*, ed. Iring Fetscher (1966). On this subject in more detail: Barbara Stollberg-Rilinger, *Der Staat als Maschine: Zur politischen Metaphorik des absoluten Fürstenstaats* (1986); Ethel Matala de Mazza, *Der verfaßte Körper: Zum Projekt einer organischen Gemeinschaft in der Politischen Romantik* (1999); Albrecht Koschorke, et al., *Der fiktive Staat: Konstruktionen des politischen Körpers in der Geschichte Europas* (2007); Stephan Meder, *Doppelte Körper im Recht* (2015), pp. 112-136.

[3] René Descartes, "Beschreibung des menschlichen Körpers und aller seiner Funktionen, ebenso von denen, die nicht von der Seele abhängen, wie von denen, die von ihr abhängig sind, außerdem über die wesentliche Ursache für die Bildung seiner Glieder", in: id., Über den Menschen (1632) sowie Beschreibung des menschlichen Körpers (1648), ed. Karl Eduard Rothschuh (1969), pp. 137-194.

> is a similarity in the rules according to which we reflect upon these two things and their causality.[4]

The "similarity" in our reflection about the State and a hand-mill stems from the fact that both are "governed by an individual absolute will". The law also has such a similarity with the machine: the law and the machine can be reflected upon in the same manner, because the State philosophy of enlightened absolutism "imagines" the law as a "mere machine [...] governed by an individual will". It is a small step to the idea of the jurist acting by order of State legislation and able by means of mechanical operation to decide any case that arises. The idea is in essence still alive today. It surfaces mostly where methodological teachings want to see subsumption or judicial syllogism as a central working technique of modern jurists.

However, if asked, experienced lawyers would respond to the question of what they think about subsumption automata or similar machines in unambiguous terms: such apparatus traditionally encountered clear rejection for two reasons. First, because the subsumption automaton metaphor arose at a particular time in history. And second, because the metaphor is itself a reflection of history. The ideal of the bureaucrat, conceptually situated at a high level, equipped with a "thinking machine", and able to solve every conceivable legal case by means of deduction is thought to have originated in eras that were shaped by "jurisprudential formalism". And what eras were they? Answering that question is difficult because there is ambiguity about the image we should have of jurisprudence in the nineteenth century.

CONFUSING INFORMATION ON THE LEGAL AUTOMATON IN THE NINETEENTH CENTURY

For more than 150 years the history of jurisprudence in Germany commenced with the strict formalism of Pandectics and led through to post-positivist concepts of methodology.

[4] Immanuel Kant, *Kritik der Urteilskraft: Text auf Grundlage der drei Originalausgaben von 1790, 1793 und 1799*, eds. Karl Vorländer and Heiner F. Klemme (7th ed.; 1990), p. 256. English version: Immanuel Kant, *Critique of Judgment*, ed. J. H. Bernard (1914), § 59.

An abbreviated account is as follows: Friedrich Carl von Savigny (1779-1861) was the most important jurist in the nineteenth century. His Historical School of Law (*Historische Rechtsschule*) greatly influenced the legal field in Germany and is still a dominant force. However, Savigny was also a pioneer of jurisprudential formalism, a form of legal positivism which demands rigorous application of the law and is characterized by detachment from everyday life and machine-like application of the law. Rudolf von Jhering (1818-1892), with his "Laws as a Means to an End" (1877), attempted to penetrate and master the social reality of civic society using new instruments in jurisprudence. For example, the introduction to the "Palandt", the most widely used commentary on the German Civil Code (BGB), states even today that in 1900, when the BGB came into effect, the "so-called conceptualization of the law was the dominant legal method" (best-known representatives: Savigny, Windscheid)". The differentiation "of concepts and their consolidation into a closed system was understood as a logical-formal process": the legal practitioner had only to "subsume the life event under the relevant legal concepts".[5]

Concepts such as formalism or positivism often go hand in hand with a certain degree of vagueness, especially since it was assumed that legal positivism was less positivistic than philosophical positivism. In order to preempt such irritations, Franz Wieacker (1908-1994), professor at Göttingen University and author of *Privatrechtsgeschichte der Neuzeit*, a leading work on the history of private law in the second half of the twentieth century, felt compelled to clarify the matter in 1967. He wrote that Savigny's jurisprudential positivism "emerged from Kant's formalism based on his critique of knowledge" and would therefore be "much more aptly termed jurisprudential formalism". Accordingly, Savigny developed a concept of law that depends on Kant's philosophical idealism. It is a position that has long been maintained and called into doubt only by recent research. This is why it was believed in the second half of the twentieth century and is still believed by some today that Savigny and

[5] See the references in Stephan Meder, "Rudolf von Jhering und der Aufstand gegen den rechtswissenschaftlichen Formalismus", *JuristenZeitung*, LXXIV (2019), p. 689 et seq.

the pandectology he co-founded had propagated a working technique that, as a "jurisprudence of concepts", degraded the jurist to a subsumption automaton.[6] However, Savigny was in fact one of the first to undertake a fundamental critique of codification and rejected any suggestion of a mechanical or machine-like application of law outright.

AUTOMATA IN THE SECOND AGE OF THE LEGAL MACHINE

It is widely believed that the automaton metaphor was introduced by the Free Law Movement (*Freirechtsbewegung*) in the early twentieth century.[7] Earlier sources dating back to the early nineteenth century show that skepticism towards a machine-based or mechanistic application of the law existed. Even then, machine-like application of the law was used pejoratively to describe a type of legal decision-making that no longer requires any human input and that slavishly adheres to a "prescribed" wording. The subsumption machine shares this pejorative connotation with Rudolf von Jhering's "judgment machine" (*Urteilsmaschine*), Hermann Kantorowicz's (1877-1940) "thinking machine" (*Denkmaschine*), and Max Weber's (1864-1920) "paragraph automaton" (*Paragraphenautomat*), into which "one throws the files at the top, together with costs and fees, so that it spits out the judgment at the bottom, along with more or less valid reasons". All these machines or automata, which will be examined more closely in the following chapters, caricature the kind of formalization where, in applying the law, judges are to repeat what is written in the law without making any additions of their own.

[6] Kyriakos N. Kotsoglou, "Subsumtionsautomat 2.0. Über die (Un-)Möglichkeit einer Algorithmisierung der Rechtserzeugung", *JuristenZeitung* LXIX (2014), pp. 451-457. On the problems of Wieacker's historical narrative, see Stephan Meder, "Franz Wieackers 'Wandlungen im Bilde der historischen Rechtsschule' neu gelesen: Ein schiefes Bild der Rechtsgeschichte?", in: *Festschrift für Albert Janssen* (forthcoming).

[7] See Clara Günzl, "Subsumtionsautomaten und -maschinen. Rechtshistorische Anmerkungen zu einem beliebten Vorwurf", *JuristenZeitung*, LXXIV (2019), pp. 180-188; Regina Ogorek, *Richterkönig oder Subsumtionsautomat? Zur Justiztheorie im 19. Jahrhundert* (1986), p. 5.

In contrast, the new "machines" are taken more seriously in terms of functions such as autonomous technical systems, legal technology, or legal tech. This development is rooted in the past as well, in this case around fifty years ago when the first indications of the dawning of a second age of legal machines became apparent. A group of legal scholars, logicians, computer scientists, and linguists attempted to establish the foundations for automated analysis of the interpretation of legislative texts. Even then, the same advantages of a technical solution to the problem were extolled that are foreshadoweded today: facilitating the judiciary's work, increasing the speed and cost-effectiveness of judgments, and excluding the private opinions of decision-makers. The goal was to develop programs which would formalize legal propositions and derive subsumptions from a formal logical comparison of Major and Minor Premises. The idea of the "subsumption automaton" was also boosted by the fact that previously frowned upon terms such as logic, derivation, or deduction could now be used without inhibition or proviso. Soon, however, it became apparent that rule-based systems could not be applied to understanding language. Everyday tasks that humans are able to perform effortlessly presented the systems with almost insurmountable difficulties. In consequence, many researchers and scholars turned away from automatic decision-making, and this period is now referred to as the "winter of artificial intelligence".[8]

Today, computers compose music and defeat humans at checkers, chess, and Go. Recent technological advances have given fresh momentum to discussions about whether legal decisions can perhaps be arrived at using automata after all. Artificial legal intelligence no longer works primarily on the basis of predefined rules, using instead large amounts of data in the form of statements of facts, case law, legal texts, commentaries, reviews of judgments, and other sources, all of which are transformed into mathematical equations and examined according to their numerical frequency in relation to a specific legal question. Like the controversial model of a judicial syllogism, however, the application of law on

[8] Ulrich Eberl, "Was ist künstliche Intelligenz - was kann sie leisten?", *Aus Politik und Geschichte: Zeitschrift der Bundeszentrale für Politische Bildung*, LXVIII (2018), p. 10.

the basis of algorithms reduces legal decisions to a purely formal act.

"Formalization" is in this context to be understood in a double sense, first as the transformation of natural language into formal language, and second as the digital deciding of legal cases. The second age of the legal machine could not properly be called that if the old skepticism about legal formalism had not given way to almost boundless optimism. In a recent interview on the future of digital justice, Philipp Otto, a futurologist and leading expert on digitalization, said: in the future, the judicial system will

> look completely different - perhaps not a single sheet of paper will be used anymore. It will probably be quite normal for people with little financial freedom and practically no legal knowledge to be able to access legal advice easily and unbureaucratically, because the processes will have been optimized so much that they will hardly incur any costs. And maybe we will laugh when we look back at this interview, because the questions will seem to be about things we long since stopped worrying over. I would find all of that very positive, and the idea makes me extremely optimistic about the future.[9]

HOW DOES LEGAL REASONING WORK?

This vision survives of one day being able to optimize legal decision-making based on formal procedures to such a degree that the solution to a legal case can simply be derived by programming in future events. All the tiresome "thinking" about law and, to take one example, about the complex interplay with ethical values, would have been dispensed with. "And perhaps we'll laugh" because such questions "will seem to be things" that have long since been settled. Any discussion of formalism, positivism, or autonomous systems always brings the past and the future, and thus history, into play. But how does legal reasoning

[9] Phillip Otto in H. Radke, „Digitale Justiz aus dem Blickwinkel des Zukunftsforschers: Interview mit Philipp Otto", *Juris*, no.12 (2019), pp. 482–483.

really work? Is there a theory that could explain how to correctly determine the significance of the facts of a case and of legal texts? What information must an autonomous system be fed with in order to be able to make decisions in place of a human? These questions of legal methodology must be asked because autonomous intelligent systems need jurists: legal experts must explain how legal reasoning works to computer scientists and programmers if they are to transform legal texts into formal language.[10]

The current literature on legal tech neglects methodological issues and seems to accentuate the concept of continental European legal reasoning. For example, a much-cited recent study on the formalization of the law (*Formalisierung des Rechts*) by autonomous systems states: "Continental European law is based on the concept of positive written law and therefore on a strict separation of the legislative process and the application of the law". The study is therefore limited to "cases in which the written law is sufficient and does not have to be supplemented by the development of the law".[11]

[10] Oliver Raabe, et al., *Recht ex machina* (2012), p. 171.

[11] Ibid., note 10 above, p. 7 et seq. with further references. According to general opinion, standard-setting or legislation is a generalizing, anticipatory regulation of a large number of similar cases - a programming of future events, primarily by government law. In contrast, the person applying the law makes a decision in an individual case, i.e. settles a unique, past and non-repeatable event. Like jurisdiction, the application of the law is not future-oriented, but merely situation-oriented. In addition, the application of the law primarily affects the particular interests of the parties involved, whereas legislation predominantly covers relationships of significance to society as a whole. Against this view, the objection has been raised that laws can only predict future behavior to a limited extent. Moreover, language is always imprecise and subject to interpretation. The goals of a statute can therefore usually only be attained through the interaction of legislation and application of the law. Moreover, the precedential effect must be taken into account even when deciding an individual case, because for reasons of the uniformity of the law, statutes must be interpreted in the same or similar manner in the same or similar cases. Furthermore, a commonality between legislation and the application of law is that in both cases it is a matter of the development of the law - of the creation of law in the sense of an independent concretization or evaluation of the person who seeks to decide a particular conflict. Thus, there is a controversy about the question if and to what extent legislation and the application of law are different. Now one feature of jurisprudential formalism is that it takes a clear position in this controversy. Classical formalism (from the era of the first machine age)

It comes as no surprise that the approach encountered vigorous resistance. Many authors doubted that a strict "separation of the legislative process and the application of the law" was possible in this context.[12] We can ask ourselves whether generally acceptable assertions can be made about the tasks of legal reasoning and legal method.

That question cannot be answered conclusively in this study. Some of the discussions about legal machines, however, can be used to highlight certain main points to which legal thinking seems to return again and again. In order to illustrate these points, it appears advisable to devise a scale that ranges from the traditional idea of codification with its strict separation of the legislative process and the application of the law at one end to the doctrine of Free Law with its assertion that each case has its own method at the other. Between these extremes of subsumption automata and sovereign judges lie, of course, many gradations and correlations, so that the thesis will be: only a dialectical combination of formal and material elements is able to do justice to the complexity of legal thinking. In the process, it is assumed that many eras have passed during which questions were raised about the relationship between automatism and evaluation, between formalism and finalism, and

is based on the premise that an authority exists that can regulate future events by means of general rules. The first thing to think of here would be the legislature, whose most prominent task, according to general opinion, is to legislate. This jurisprudential formalism thus draws a sharp dividing line between the application of law and legislation: the state legislator alone is authorized to regulate future events according to its sovereign will, while the function of the application of law is limited to helping to enforce the rules by way of rulings - ideally without any active intervention. It was, of course, disputed early on that it is at all possible to draw such dividing lines between legislation and the application of law (as a more recent example, one need only refer to the engaging discussion of the topic by Matthias Jestaedt, who, like so many, admittedly also cannot do without the assertion of a "subsumption-positivist conceptual jurisprudence", in: Hans-Uwe Erichsen and Dirk Ehlers (eds.), *Allgemeines Verwaltungsrecht* (14th ed.; 2010), p. 334 et seq. with references from the field of public law). Raabe et al., note 10 above, ignore this discussion when they believe they can retreat to the position of a continental European "subsumption automaton" (see chapter 2, note 14; chapter 4, note 13; chapter 7, note 9).

[12] See, for example, the criticism of Axel Adrian, "Der Richterautomat ist möglich – Semantik ist nur eine Illusion", *Rechtstheorie,* XLVIII (2017), p. 82 et seq.; Kotsoglou, note 6 above.

between stricter and freer elements in the forming of the law and the finding of judgments: the strata underlying the present discussions are remnants of Antiquity, Byzantium, the Middle Ages, Renaissance, Rationalism, the Historical School of Law, and Pandectics with all their ramifications.

The first topic selected for discussion is "conceptual jurisprudence", which primarily means Pandectics and the first half of the nineteenth century, in which this approach is agreed to have developed. That the Free Law Movement is commonly thought to have introduced the topos of the subsumption automaton has already been indicated. It is true that especially during the period of the doctrine of Free Law, the concept of subsumption automatism was put into opposition to conceptual jurisprudence and jurisprudential formalism, fighting the idea of a machine-like application of the law. However, the term "conceptual jurisprudence" had already been coined by Rudolf von Jhering, and he rejected judgment machines and a logical-mechanical application of the law, a position which was later taken up and intensified by the doctrine of Free Law. Therefore, our attention turns first to Jhering's understanding of conceptual jurisprudence and judgment machines.

Chapter 1
Rudolf von Jhering: Vaucanson's Duck as "Judgment Machine"

Jacques de Vaucanson (1709-1782), a French engineer and inventor, dreamed of building an artificial human. He caused a sensation when he constructed a human automaton - a mechanical flutist he presented in 1738 at the Académie des Sciences in Paris. His true masterpiece, however, was an automated duck that could flap its wings, quack, and consume and even digest food. This duck therefore not only imitated the external movement of creatures, a feat accomplished by many others at the time; it also simulated the dignity of the organic and therefore of "life". In a letter to Abbé Desfontaines (1685-1745) in 1738, Vaucanson described his invention, not without pride, thus:

> The Duck stretches out its Neck to take Corn out of your Hand; it swallows it, digests it, and discharges it digested by the usual Passage. [...] The Matter digested in the Stomach is conducted by Pipes, (as in an Animal in the Guts) quite to the Anus, where there is a Sphincter that lets it out.[1]

When Gaston Bachelard (1884-1962), the French philosopher interested in the theory of science, wrote an

[1] See Johann Andreas Erdmann Maschenbaur, "Des Herrn Vaucanson Schreiben an den Herrn Abt D.F.", in: Maschenbaur (ed.), *Beschreibung eines mechanischen Kunst-Stucks und Avtomatischen Flöten-Spielers* (1748), p. 21. From the extensive literature on Vaucanson's constructions, examples can be found in Jessica Riskin, "The Defecating Duck, or, the Ambiguous Origins of Artificial Life", *Critical Inquiry*, XXIX (2003), pp. 599-633; Jochen Büchel, *Psychologie der Materie: Vorstellungen und Bildmuster von der Assimilation von Nahrung im 17. und 18. Jahrhundert unter besonderer Berücksichtigung des Paracelsismus* (2005), pp. 19–21; Carsten Priebe, Vito von Eichborn, *Eine Reise durch die Aufklärung: Maschinen, Manufakturen und Mätressen; die Abenteuer von Vaucansons Ente oder die Suche nach künstlichem Leben* (2007).

essay on "the myth of digestion" two centuries later, he stated: "Digestion is the origin of the strongest kind of realism".[2] Might this "realism" perhaps be the reason for the fascination that Vaucanson's construction exerted on Jhering? In the first volume of his *Law as a Means to the End,* originally published in 1877 in German under the title *Der Zweck im Recht,* Jhering referenced the duck in the context of the basic question that concerns the relationship between law and justice: can detailed legislation replace the "mind of the judge"? Can a legal decision be determined through formal-logical and mechanical methods of applying the law? "Experience has judged here also", wrote Jhering, probably thinking of the nearly 20,000 laws with which the General State Laws for the Prussian States of 1794 [*Preußisches Allgemeines Landrecht*] attempted to reduce the juristic need for discernment to a minimum.

Jhering doubted the claims to reality for a mechanical application of the law. He did not believe that the judge could be provided with "detailed regulations for every case, juristic recipes for the decision of all possible law-suits, which [would] free him from all further searching".

> The impossibility of seeing beforehand the infinite variety and manifold formation of cases, stamps this attempt of absolutely fixing the judicial decision as a wrong one from the start. The idea in the mind of the author is to make the application of the law a purely mechanical thing, in which judicial thinking should be made superfluous by the law. We are reminded of the duck constructed by Vaucanson, which carried out the process of digestion mechanically; the case is thrown into the judging machine in front, and it comes out again as a judgment behind.[3]

[2] Gaston Bachelard, "Der Mythos der Verdauung", in: Bachelard, *Die Bildung des wissenschaftlichen Geistes: Beitrag zu einer Psychoanalyse der objektiven Erkenntnis* (2nd ed.; 1978), pp. 251-268; English Translation: Gaston Bachelard, *The Formation of the Scientific Mind: A Contribution to a Psychoanalysis of Objective Knowledge* (2002), p. 172.

[3] Rudolf von Jhering, *Der Zweck im Recht: Band I* (3rd ed.; 1893), p. 394. English translation, Rudolf von Jhering, *Law as a Means to an End* (1999), p. 295.

Jhering painted a drastic, even crude, picture of a judgment machine. It must be remembered his intention was not to diminish the worth of judges when he likened their work to the digestion of animals and the judgment to excrement. Such parallels were supposed only to alienate those who postulated the determination of legal decision by general legal rules, by law or dogmatics. Jhering's judgment machine is rather to be understood in the wider context of his critique of the legal systems that became famous under the term "Begriffsjurisprudenz" [jurisprudence of concepts].

JHERING'S ATTACK ON "BEGRIFFSJURISPRUDENZ"

The first steps in the critique of legal formalism and the mechanical application of the law was Jhering's coining of the term "Begriffsjurisprudenz", a label that is still used in German legal studies. The controversy surrounding this jurisprudence of concepts has resonated in countries outside Germany as well, especially in the United States. Everything began with the obituary Jhering wrote to mark Savigny's death in 1861, published in the year of his death. The tribute contained some key elements of Jhering's legal critique when he wrote that Savigny had brought about an "alienation between theory and practice" and had underestimated "the importance of the human power of action" for the creation of law, while also disapproving of the "apparatus of general ideas" that "Savigny considered necessary to set in motion against his opponents".[4]

In the initially anonymous "Vertraulichen Briefe über die heutige Jurisprudenz" (1861-1866) and the "Plaudereien eines Romanisten" (1880), Jhering expanded on his critique. His "fantasy image" - a satirical account of the jurisprudence

[4] Rudolf von Jhering, "Friedrich Karl von Savigny", *Jherings Jahrbücher für die Dogmatik des bürgerlichen Rechts,* V (1861), pp. 354-377. Also see: Jhering, *Gesammelte Aufsätze aus den Jahrbüchern für die Dogmatik des heutigen römischen und deutschen Privatrechts* (1882), II, pp. 13, 14, 10; Jhering, *Der Kampf ums Recht (1872)* (5th ed.; 1977), pp. 7–9 (Kritik des Vergleichs von Recht und Sprache; "nur das Gesetz, d.h. die absichtliche [...] Tat der Staatsgewalt" könne das Recht wirklich fortbilden und reformieren) [criticizing the comparison of law and language; "only the law, i.e., the deliberate [...] act of state power" can truly develop and reform law] (passages here are own translations).

of concepts that he published a few years later in "Im juristischen Begriffshimmel" gained some prominence. Jhering used dialogue to outline Kant's philosophy, according to which "the world that you deem to have perceived" exists only as "imagination" and in the shape of "forms of your subjective view". The concepts derived from these "forms" do not "mix well with life, they require a world of their own, in which they exist on their own, removed from all interaction with life".[5] In fact, according to Kant, legal action makes real a rule of reason whose object "is not encountered at all apart from the concept". Thus, freedom is also a "pure concept of reason" of which "no adequate example can be given in any possible experience". When Jhering disputed the incompatibility of concept and life, he first criticized a kind of "idealism" which, like a machine, seeks to banish reality from law as far as is possible. On the basis of a philosophy which is oriented towards concepts of reason, even the circumstances of an individual case can no longer confound the law. Kant, for example, has to accept

[5] The "Vertraulichen Briefe" [Confidential Letters about the Jurisprudence of Today] and the "Plaudereien eines Romanisten" [Conversations of a Romanist] are included (along with the final chapter "Wieder auf Erden") in: *Scherz und Ernst in der Jurisprudenz. Eine Weihnachtsgabe für das juristische Publikum* (9th ed.; 1904). The text most important for the critique of conceptual jurisprudence, "Im juristischen Begriffshimmel" (pp. 247-333), with its critical remarks on Kant's "philosophical idealism" ["philosophischem Idealismus"] for which "the real world is mere appearance, mere conception of the subject" [für den die reale Welt bloßer Schein, bloße Vorstellung des Subjekts ist], is also found there (ibid., p. 274). Again and again, Jhering complains about the loss of reality of idealism, its distance from practice and from "everyday life". Elsewhere he states: The "*mons idealis*" provides "the theorist with the gift of ideal thinking" ["dem Theoretiker die Gabe des idealen Denkens"], which is based on the ability "to free oneself from the preconditions of their practical realization when thinking about juridical things" [sich bei dem Denken juristischer Dinge von den Voraussetzungen ihrer praktischen Verwirklichung frei zu machen.], (ibid., p. 273). "Like the eagle soaring into the clouds", the conceptual jurist "soars into the regions of ideal thought and bathes himself here in the pure ether of thought, unconcerned about the real world that lies far below him and is removed from his view" ["Dem Adler gleich, der sich in die Wolken erhebt", schwingt sich der Begriffsjurist "in die Regionen des idealen Denkens und badet sich hier in dem reinen Gedankenäther, unbekümmert um die reale Welt, die tief unter ihm liegt und seinen Blicken entrückt ist."], (ibid., p. 274). The frequent use of terms such as "real" or "real world" attracted considerable interest among early legal realists in the United States (see chapter 2 below).

that the highest law can lead to the highest infringement of the law: *summum ius summa est iniuria.*[6]

Jhering's reservations towards the jurisprudence of concepts were not limited to a critique of Kant's philosophical idealism: He identified the idealism with the thinking of leading minds of the Historical School of Law, anticipating an approach taken by many later authors. Jhering also outlined other distinctive elements that are identified as attributes of jurisprudential formalism to this day, including the claim that conceptual jurists simply derive the decision from concepts by way of deduction and with no assessment of the consequences. The equation of jurisprudence with mathematics, as well as the accusations of scholasticism and positivism, are already present. Jhering further pointed out that the jurisprudence of concepts is based on the idea that law is a system committed solely to logic, which as a "*mos geometricus*" develops its principles independently of social reality.[7] Given this background, it is not surprising

[6] The passages mentioned in this paragraph can be found in Kant, *Kritik der reinen Vernunft* (2d ed.; 1787), B 504, 506; Kant, *Metaphysik der Sitten* (1797), in: *Werkausgabe* (10th ed.; 1993), VIII, pp. 326, 342. Although Kant repeatedly used the machine metaphor in his works, and although he excluded consideration of equity [Billigkeit] and thought that judges should not decide according to indeterminate conditions, he cannot be counted an apologist for a machine application of law. He characterized the "determining power of judgment" [bestimmende Urteilskraft] relevant for the legal decision not as a formal-logical operation, but as a capacity that is independent of the intellect. Judging does not only require 'theoretical' abilities, but is also a 'practical' activity, i.e. the specific of "talent" and "maternal wit" [Mutterwitz], the "lack of which no school can replace" [Mangel keine Schule ersetzen kann]. For details, see Stephan Meder, *Urteilen: Elemente von Kants reflektierender Urteilskraft in Savignys Lehre von der juristischen Entscheidungs- und Regelfindung* (1999), pp. 27–34.

[7] At the center of Jhering's criticism of conceptual jurisprudence is the accusation that it is distanced from practical life, cf. "Juristischer Begriffshimmel", note 5 above, p. 253 (Herrschaft von Rechtslogik und reiner Wissenschaft), p. 273 (Fragen der Anwendung bleiben außer Betracht), p. 274 (Beschränkung auf das logische Denken; Gleichung von Jurisprudenz und Mathematik; Scholastik- und Positivismus-Vorwurf). See also the "Wiener Antrittsvorlesung (1868)", in: Okko Behrends, *Ist die Jurisprudenz eine Wissenschaft? Jherings Wiener Antrittsvorlesung vom 16. Oktober 1868* (1998), pp. 52-54. All these keywords are taken up by notable scholars and so will shape jurisprudence in the twentieth century. The first to be mentioned must be Franz Wieacker, who also combines the mechanistic world view of rational natural law and enlightened rational law with the legal criticism of, for example, Savigny

that Jhering often drew on the image of the machine in the application of law. Thus, as early as 1868, he commented on judges passing verdicts under the title "The Positivistic Jurist - A Mindless Cog in the Machinery of Law":

> However, even worse than this external dependence is another danger that threatens jurisprudence not externally but internally: the danger of internal, intellectual dependence, the danger of giving oneself and one's thinking and feeling to the barren, dead law, of becoming a will-less and uncaring piece of the legal machinery, in short, of escaping from one's own thinking.[8]

At first glance, this statement differs from Jhering's reflections on Vaucanson's duck and on the "judgment machine": in it, the legal system as such and the entire administration of justice is apparently mere machinery. However, in the strict sense it is not possible to separate jurists and the legal system, for it is precisely this "machinery" that also reduces the individual jurist or judge to a "will-less and unfeeling piece", to a mere component or "cog" in the machine.

FROM JURISPRUDENCE OF CONCEPTS TO CRITIQUE OF LEGAL FORMALISM

Academic opinion tends to divide Jhering's work into two periods: his 'jurisprudence of concepts' period and a later phase of critical writing beginning in the early 1860s. This view is being revised as recent research has shown that Jhering's thinking had incorporated elements of critique as

or Puchta. See Franz Wieacker, *Privatrechtsgeschichte der Neuzeit: Unter besonderer Berücksichtigung der deutschen Entwicklung* (2d ed.; 1967), p. 401 (so habe sich "der wissenschaftliche Begriff vom Lebensgrund abgelöst und nur mehr intellektuelle Existenz"). See also the translation: Franz Wieacker, *A History of Private Law in Europe: With Particular Reference to Germany* (1995).

[8] Jhering, "Wiener Antrittsvorlesung", note 7 above, p. 50 et seq. Jhering's critical remarks on the "judgment machine" [Urteilsmaschine] and "legal machinery" [Rechtsmaschine] must not be confused with his praise of mechanism in ancient Roman law (on such misunderstandings, widespread especially in literary studies, see the references in chapter 5, note 4).

early as 1844. On the other hand, Jhering himself created the sense that there was an early and a late period in his work, for example when he spoke of a turning point or an about-face, of "a strange transformation in my whole outlook". Taking such autobiographical statements and the traditional division of Jhering's work into two phases at face value inevitably leads to the conclusion that, with his critique of both conceptual jurisprudence and the machine metaphor, Jhering anticipated essential arguments which opponents of jurisprudential formalism will take up.

Jhering, who had been teaching in Göttingen since 1872, rarely used the term 'formal' in that sense. Although he does speak of a "formal independence of law" and sometimes of "formalism",[9] he mostly associated them with questions of form and formal rigor, as they find expression, for example, in formal requirements. It is widely recognized today that Jhering's reflections on the functions of form in law and its connection with freedom constitute a milestone in legal historical research. His critique culminated in the famous phrase, "Form is the enemy of arbitrariness, the twin sister of liberty".[10] In other words, Jhering did not understand "form" only in a pejorative sense, and even defended the constraint of form in law against its critics. His verdict on the "formalism of concepts", on the other hand, was unyielding. "Form in law" and "jurisprudence of concepts" must therefore be carefully separated as areas of interest.

Jhering's critique of the jurisprudence of concepts and the Historical School of Law was very well received in scholarly circles, and he was soon celebrated as the "most vigorous champion" of the movement that had restored jurisprudence to its social foundations. He rightly observed "that jurisprudence - similar to logic and mathematics - is a

[9] Rudolf von Jhering, *Geist des römischen Rechts auf den verschiedenen Stufen seiner Entwicklung: Zweiter Theil, Erste Abtheilung* (4th ed.; 1880), e.g. § 24, p. 22; Jhering, *Geist des römischen Rechts auf den verschiedenen Stufen seiner Entwicklung: Zweiter Theil, Zweite Abtheilung* (4th ed.; 1883), §45, pp. 470 and 480; § 45a, pp. 504, 519.

[10] Jhering, note 9 above, p. 471. For details, see Peter Oestmann, "Die Zwillingsschwester der Freiheit. Die Form im Recht als Problem der Rechtsgeschichte", in: Oestmann (ed.), *Zwischen Formstrenge und Billigkeit: Forschungen zum vormodernen Zivilprozeß* (2009), pp. 20-23.

formal science, that it merely develops the forms of human thought, that it [...] is devoid of reality".[11] Yet Jhering himself was barely able to break free from formalistic ideas, as seen, for example, in the fact that he approaches the material elements of law with great caution. In "Geist des römischen Rechts" he admitted that "the material content of law is of the greatest influence on its realization". However, he states, the jurist has "no power" over the substantive adequacy; only the legislator has such power, and the legislator's method is also concerned with adequacy. This concern is not of a material, but only of a "*formal* nature".[12] Scholars have puzzled over how this dichotomy can be explained. According to Rudolf Müller-Erzbach, it may, "originate partly from the fact that Jhering's temperament was less suited to a systematic approach". The explanation offered by French sociologist Georges Gurvitch was not quite as kind, when he stated that Jhering's "only merit" was "to oppose the doctrines of his predecessors".[13]

[11] Julius Ofner, *Studien sozialer Jurisprudenz* (1894), p. 17; Karl Georg Wurzel, *Das juristische Denken: Studie* (1904), p. 6 (emphasis added). The findings lead to the demand for greater freedom for judges, which the doctrine of Free Law will then take as the most radical direction in the contemporary methodological debate. Even earlier, Oskar Bülow held that the law and the judge share legislative competence. See id, *Gesetz und Richteramt* (1885), p. 41. Prior to Bülow, Franz Adickes in *Zur Lehre von den Rechtsquellen: Insbesondere über die Vernunft und die Natur der Sache als Rechtsquellen und über das Gewohnheitsrecht* (1872), elevated the judge's "subjective reason" to a source of law. Jhering also acknowledged a certain "productivity" on the part of the judge. See his Vienna inaugural lecture, note 7 above, pp. 88–90; however, he merely invoked the "history of all peoples and times" [Geschichte aller Völker und Zeiten]. Parallel to the polemic against conceptual jurisprudence, he was primarily concerned with a rejection of all those who want to see in "the judge only a piece of the legal machinery" [Richter nur ein Stück der Rechtsmaschine]. Ibid., p. 89.

[12] Jhering, note 9 above, §38, p. 325 (emphasis in original).

[13] Rudolf Müller-Erzbach, *Die Hinwendung der Rechtswissenschaft zum Leben und was sie hemmt* (1939), p. 21 (sometimes also referring to the "disjointedness of the 19th century" [Zerissenheit des 19. Jahrhunderts]); Georges Gurvitch, *Grundzüge der Soziologie des Rechts* (2d ed.; 1974), p. 73 (regarding Jhering's rejection of the law-language comparison, see the references in chapter 2 at note 4).

SUCCESS OF JHERING'S LEGAL CRITIQUE IN THE UNITED STATES

In comparative law, the subsumption automaton is a much-used metaphor for describing the differences between "civil" and "common" law. As early as 1905, Julius Hatschek (1872-1926), a scholar of constitutional, administrative, and international law, wrote: "In accordance with the principle of separation of powers, the judge [in Germany] must be a 'subsumption automaton'," because otherwise he would assume legislative powers. Similar assertions can be found in Max Weber's work or – after the Second World War – in the works of Konrad Zweigert and more recent scholars.[14] The reason for recourse to the subsumption automaton is easy to find as it embodies the image of two opposing "legal circles", one of which is understood to be determined by statutory law in the form of codifications and the other by "judge-made-law" in the form of precedents. Against this background, it may appear surprising that Jhering's critique of the jurisprudence of concepts was well received in "common law" countries and, in particular, in the United States. For example, the pioneer of the sociology of law

[14] Julius Hatschek, *Englisches Staatsrecht mit Berücksichtigung der für Schottland und Irland geltenden Sonderheiten. Vol. I: Die Verfassung* (1905), pp. 157, 154; Max Weber, "Politische Gemeinschaften", in id, *Wirtschaft und Gesellschaft: Grundriß der verstehenden Soziologie,* ed. Johannes Winkelmann (5th ed.; 1985), pp. 514–868: Thus, modern capitalism was able to develop "where *either*, as in England, the practical shaping of the law actually lay in the hands of the advocates, who, in the service of their clientele, i.e. the interested capitalist parties, devised the appropriate forms of business, and from among them then emerged the judges, strictly bound to 'precedents', i.e. to *calculable* schemes. *Or* where the judge, as in the bureaucratic state with its rational laws, is more or less an automaton of paragraphs into which the files are thrown at the top together with the costs and fees, so that at the bottom he spits out the verdict together with the more or less sound reasoning: - [a machine] whose functioning is thus in any case by and large *calculable*" [wo *entweder*, wie in England, die praktische [...] im großen und ganzen *kalkulierbar* ist], (p. 826). Konrad Zweigert says: "The judge appeared to legal positivism like a kind of automaton into which one puts the case and which, after a gentle hum of the brain, brings to light the decision correctly tailored and ready to hand. And the English world still sees the judge in the continental legal state in this way; miraculously, not without a certain envy" [Der Richter erschien [...] nicht ohne einen gewissen Neid]. Zweigert, "Zum richterlichen Charisma in einer ethisierten Rechtsordnung", in: *Festgabe für Carlo Schmid zum 65. Geburtstag: Dargebracht von Freunden Schülern und Kollegen,* ed. T. Eschenburg (1962), p. 303.

and legal philosopher Roscoe Pound (1870-1964) explained the connections between jurisprudential formalism, the jurisprudence of concepts, and the mechanical application of law from a United States perspective in his "Mechanical Jurisprudence" of 1908. In it, Pound criticized a type of jurisprudence that was primarily concerned with predictability – a mechanical jurisprudence that was more interested in the beauty of its logical constructions than in the relevance of the results to life and justice: "Principles were no longer resorted to in order to make rules to fit cases. The rules were at hand in a fixed and final form, and cases were to be fitted to the rules".[15]

Pound did not conceal the fact that Jhering was his most important reference: "Ihering was the pioneer in the work of superseding this jurisprudence of conceptions (*Begriffsjurisprudenz*) by a jurisprudence of results (*Wirklichkeitsjurisprudenz*)". The assertion that the Historical School of Law had shown a certain dependence on the philosophy of idealism can also be found in Pound: "If we adopt an idealistic interpretation of legal history and conceive of the development of law as a gradual unfolding of Kant's idea of right [...], we shall understand the position of the historical school".[16]

[15] Roscoe Pound, "Mechanical jurisprudence", *Columbia Law Review*, VIII (1908), p. 607. Similarly, Albert Kocourek (1875-1952) explained the term "conceptual jurisprudence" by saying: "In its worst sense, it attempts to apply a rigorous logic to new situations [...] The lawyer and the judge who operate with legal ideas in this blind denial of the facts well may be compared to 'the physician who preferred that his patients should die by rule rather than recover contrary to it'". Kocourek, "Formal Relation Between Law and Discretion", *Illinois Law Review*, IX (1914), p. 238 (along these lines see Benjamin N. Cardozo, *The Nature of the Judicial Process* (1921), p. 102). As early testimony to the great attention paid to Jhering in the English-speaking world, see Alphonse Rivier, "Rudolf Von Jhering and Bernhard Windscheid", *The Juridical Review*, V (1893), pp. 1–12.

[16] Pound, note 15 above, p. 610 (emphasis in original). Elsewhere, Pound emphasized that Jhering was the first to cast doubt on the "logical deductions" of the Historical School of Law, which separated the jurist "from the actual life of today". Pound, *The Spirit of the Common Law* (1921), pp. 203–205. For more on this, see David M. Rabban, *Law's history: American Legal Thought and the Transatlantic Turn to History* (2013), p. 114. See also Pound, *The Spirit of the Common Law*, p. 153 (on the connections between conceptual jurisprudence and philosophical idealism). Like Pound, Albert Kocourek relied primarily on Jhering's "Scherz und

Jhering's profound impact on legal discourse in the United States has often been noted. For instance, the political scientist and philosopher Arthur F. Bentley (1870-1957) suggested that anyone who wants to understand the social function of law must have read Jhering's Zweck im Recht [purpose in law] "page for page". The real ground-breaker in the United States "revolt against formalism" is, of course, the venerable judge and legal theorist Oliver Wendell Holmes (1841-1935). Thanks to his careful record-keeping, it is widely known that Holmes had read Jhering.[17] The main target of Holmes' objection was the "classical legal thought" of Christopher Columbus Langdell (1826-1906), Dean of the Harvard Law School for 25 years. According to Holmes, Langdell saw the law as a system of unchangeable principles from which the judge could derive a decision according to the rules of logic.[18] The "revolt against formalism" gained

Ernst in der Jurisprudenz", note 5 above. He emphasized that Jhering's criticism "has no special relation to code countries". Kocourek, note 15 above, p. 235. This deserves emphasis given the conventional distinction between "civil law" and "common law". The shared point of view is the formalism critique, which revolves around the question of whether rights of a decision can be predetermined by means of binding forms at all. This was questioned, for example, by Ernst Kantorowicz, who thought that justice would only reveal itself in the immanence of a concrete judgment situation, that is, only in the judge's verdict (see chapter 3). As an aside, it should be noted that Pound also referred to Kantorowicz's critique of formalism in Pound, note 15 above, p. 607. See also Katharina Isabel Schmidt, "Der 'Formalismus-Mythos' im deutschen und amerikanischen Rechtsdenken des frühen 20. Jahrhunderts", *Der Staat,* LIII (2014), pp. 445–473. In particular, the United States protest against legal formalism, discussed below, makes clear that the problems negotiated here concern common law and civil law alike.

17 Arthur Fisher Bentley, *The Process of Government* (1908), p. 57. See further the chapter on "Jhering and the Kingdom of Justice on Earth" in Jerome Frank, *Law and the Modern Mind* (1931), pp. 217-221, 279-280; also see *The Legal Conscience: Selected Papers of Felix S. Cohen,* ed. Lucy Kramer Cohen (1960), p. 113 ("surely von Jhering's critique of the jurisprudence of concepts gave a worthy start to the laboratories of Holmes, Oliphant, Llewellyn, and even Jerome Frank"). Gerhard Casper, *Juristischer Realismus und politische Theorie im amerikanischen Rechtsdenken* (1967), p. 14; Mathias W. Reimann, "Holmes' Common Law and German Legal Science", in Robert W. Gordon (ed.), *The Legacy of Oliver Wendell Holmes, Jr* (1992), pp. 101–104. See also the comparative appreciation of the approaches of Holmes and Jhering in: Martha G. White, *Social Thought in America: The Revolt Against Formalism* (1949), pp. 15–18; Brian Z. Tamanaha, *A Realistic Theory of Law* (2017), pp. 19–21.

18 Oliver Wendell Holmes, "Book Notices: A Selection of Cases on the

further impetus from a series of writings produced in the early days of *Critical Legal Studies* when Duncan Kennedy and Morton J. Horwitz, for example, again argued against moves to disconnect the law from social reality by limiting it to logical thinking and literalism.[19]

Recently, however, a number of voices have called into question "the caricature of Langdell as a simplistic formalist", for example. They argue that the protagonists of "classical legal thought" did not view the law as a closed system that could be controlled by deduction and logic; they claim that closer examination of Langdell's work shows that the critics of formalism can find support for their arguments only in an insignificantly small part of his work. At this stage, the motives and goals of the critics of a mechanistic jurisprudence are moved into the spotlight along with the argument that the accusation of formalism often has more to do with certain of the critics' own ideological and political interests than with the criticized works themselves.[20] Accordingly, one of the many inconsistencies in formalism accusations is that the criticized authors themselves often felt that they had struggled with formalism and had overcome

Law of Contracts, with a Summary of the Topics covered by the Cases, by C. C. Langdell", *The American Law Review*, XIV (1880).

[19] Duncan Kennedy, "Legal Formality", *The Journal of Legal Studies*, II (1973). Kennedy conceives "formality" as a "mechanical application of rules" (p. 358), with Jhering being an important guarantor for him (pp. 353, 355, 360); Kennedy, "The Disenchantment of Logically Formal Legal Rationality: Or, Max Weber's Sociology in the Genealogy of the Contemporary Mode of Western Legal Thought", *Hastings Law Journal*, LV (2004) ("Savigny developed a positivist version of normative formalism", repeatedly citing Wieacker. The problem with this work, then, is that, certainly for lack of translations of the recent literature, it harkens back to the outdated critique of a supposed conceptual jurisprudence); Morton J. Horwitz, "The Rise of Legal Formalism", *The American Journal of Legal History*, XIX (1975) (looking specifically at United States events). By *"critical"*, the founders of *Critical Legal Studies* also aimed primarily at a critique of legal formalism.

[20] Roman J. Hoyos, "Beyond Classical Legal Thought: Law and Governance in Postbellum America", in Sally E. Hadden and Alfred L. Brophy (eds.), *A Companion to American Legal History* (2013), p. 89; Brian Z. Tamanaha, *Beyond the Formalist-Realist Divide: The Role of Politics in Judging* (2010), pp. 45, 44. As a blatant example, consider the way NS jurisprudence instrumentalized the formalism charge and appropriated the concept of "life" for its own purposes (see chapter 3 at note 12).

it. The leading figures of the Historical School of Law often shared this standpoint, as will be discussed below.

SUMMARY AND OUTLOOK

Jhering recognized that a philosophy of law guided by concepts of reason inevitably runs counter to the needs of modern practice. This is especially true of philosophical idealism with its theoretical basis in epistemology and its attempts to limit the law to its formal aspects. However, the reasons that Kant, along with most scholars of the Law of Reason, sought to exclude material aspects as far as possible are not just epistemological; they are also constitutional. Jhering's requirement that life's necessities be taken into account demands that jurists have a degree of formative authority that cannot be reconciled with enlightened absolutism's concept of the sovereignty. It is therefore prudent to divide Jhering's critique of the law into two separate categories. To the extent that his theory refers to philosophical idealism, little stands in the way. Kant's theory of the sources of law is no more able to do justice to the problems of modern legal practice than those of Hobbes, Pufendorf (1632-1694), or Bodin. This contrasts with the claim that Savigny or Puchta (1798-1846) devoted themselves to philosophical idealism, an assertion for which no evidence can be found in the sources. The Historical School of Law is able to concede to jurisprudence a degree of formative authority that Kant and other proponents of Secular Natural Law must reject. Its openness to equity [Billigkeit], its generous theory of interpretation, and its plural theory of the source of law will be further discussed below.

The real reason for Jhering's ambivalence can probably be found in his changing understanding of the sources of law. While he certainly did advocate a closer link between jurisprudence and social reality, he was also an ardent admirer of Bismarck and an advocate of a statist understanding of the sources of law. As a result, he quickly closed the ports of entry he opened for "everyday life": jurists have no authority over material adequacy; such authority is possessed only by the legislator.[21] The problem, then, lies in the fact that Savigny's multi-layered theory of legal sources, with its distinction between a technical and a political element, not only goes beyond the concept of "reality jurisprudence" that Jhering advocated, but is also "more modern" precisely in view of the latest understanding of the "multiplicity of legally legitimated controlling factors."[22] All in all, the name of Jhering is associated with a twofold coincidence of "civil law" and "common law": first, the critique of "mechanical jurisprudence" or legal formalism, and second, the current debate about the justification of this critique. Jhering certainly overshot the mark with his attacks on the "jurisprudence of concepts" and unfairly denigrated the teachings of his predecessors. This is also demonstrated by the fact that Savigny and Puchta had already declared themselves opponents of a mechanical application of law and had emphatically demanded a "de-automation" of jurisprudence. Nonetheless, this in no way denies that Jhering accomplished considerable feats in numerous areas of his subject. Despite all ambiguities and misinterpretations, the same applies to his critique of formalism.

[21] Jhering, note 9 above, § 38, p. 325; id., note 4 above, pp. 7–9. An ambivalence can also be seen in the fact that Jhering considers a control of results to be necessary, but is opposed to equity [Billigkeit], which is so important for the assessment of the consequences of a decision. The examples could be extended.

[22] 'More modern' also because Savigny understands the relations between formal and material, between technical and political elements as a complex interplay and basic condition of all law (more on this in chapter 6). His theory of law lies beyond the conventional divisions, the overcoming of which has recently been called for again, see e.g. Tamanaha, note 20 above.

Chapter 2
Hermann U. Kantorowicz: "Armed Only With a Thinking Machine"

At the beginning of the twentieth century, Jhering with his critique of jurisprudence of concepts was celebrated as a pioneer of the school of thought that turned jurisprudence right side up, from its head back onto its feet. According to Hermann Kantorowicz, Jhering should take "the place of honor in the hearts of German jurists that is still reserved for Savigny". In Kantorowicz's view, Jhering had not only tackled the Historical School of Law "with dramatic results", but had also "fought against his own works with humor and gravity". Only a "full and systematic development" of his "*thoughts*" would represent "in other countries as well as in Germany – the very essence of the Free Law Movement".[1]

CRITIQUE OF JURISPRUDENTIAL FORMALISM BY THE DOCTRINE OF FREE LAW

What are these thoughts that the doctrine of Free Law wants to develop? Foremost is undoubtedly the term "jurisprudence of concepts", which Eugen Ehrlich, Hermann Kantorowicz, and Ernst Fuchs took as the starting point of their legal criticism, for it had been Jhering who had initiated the departure from a so-called "literal and conceptual jurisprudence unconcerned with the needs of everyday life".[2] The German Free Law School, however, does

[1] Hermann U. Kantorowicz, "Die Epochen der Rechtswissenschaft", *Die Tat*, VI (1914), pp. 345-361; reprinted in Helmut Coing and Gerhard Immel (eds.), *Hermann Kantorowicz - Rechtshistorische Schriften* (1970), pp. 1-14, 14 (emphasis added; hereinafter cited as EdR).

[2] Kantorowicz, *Rechtswissenschaft und Soziologie* (1911), in: id, *Rechtswissenschaft und Soziologie: ausgewählte Schriften zur Wissenschaftslehre*, ed. Thomas Würtenberger (1962), p. 125 et seq.; id, "Was ist uns Savigny?", *Recht und Wirtschaft*, I (1912), p. 53 et seq.;

not stop at the "jurisprudence of concepts"; it searches for alternatives and finds them in terms such as pandectology, formal jurisprudence, or the formal-logical method. Indeed, it deserves credit for subjecting the concept of jurisprudential formalism to closer scrutiny for the first time, even if in the process it only returns to those definitions that Jhering had already identified. The following keywords and terms shall suffice here: deduction, subsumption, logic, emphasis on theory, remoteness from practical considerations, positivism, loss of social reality, remoteness from "everyday life", geometry, conceptual mathematics, determinism, scholasticism, idealism.[3] However, the doctrine of Free Law applies these characteristics not only to writers from the Historical School or Pandectistics, but also to the German Civil Code of 1900 (BGB) and to the practice of applicable law: "Formalism [...] infests the whole of law as a formal-logical method".[4]

It is probable that Jhering would have rejected the radical anti-formalism propagated by the doctrine of Free Law. Support for this belief can be found in the fact that, during the second phase of his work, he frequently alternated between condemning and praising "formalism". The doctrine of Free Law even criticized him for adhering too strongly to formalism and for not having brought his work to a conclusion.[5] One of the most important authors in the Free Law Movement was scholar Hermann U. Kantorowicz (1877-1940), professor of criminal law, history of law and philosophy of law, who had emigrated to the United

id, "Iherings Bekehrung", *Deutsche Richterzeitung*, VI (1914), pp. 84-87; Ernst Fuchs, *Juristischer Kulturkampf* (1912), p. 4; id, *Jhering und die Freirechtsbewegung* (1918/19), in: Fuchs, *Gerechtigkeitswissenschaft* (1965), pp. 181-191; Eugen Ehrlich, "Die juristische Logik", *Archiv für die civilistische Praxis*, CXV (1917), cited here from the 2d ed. (1918), pp. 135, 295.

[3] Kantorowicz, note 2 above, p. 120; Ehrlich, note 2 above, pp. 134 et seq., 294 et seq.; Fuchs, *Begriffsjurisprudenz* (1912), in *Gesammelte Schriften über Freirecht und Rechtsreform*, ed. Albert S. Foulkes (1973), II, p. 50 et seq. (see there for a differentiation between "formalism of concepts" and "formalism of form").

[4] Fuchs, note 3 above, p. 51.

[5] See for example Ernst Fuchs, *Jhering und die Freirechtsbewegung* (1918/19), in Fuchs, note 2 above, pp. 185-186.

States after being dismissed from his position in 1933. His most widely respected text, the "Battle for Legal Science" ["Kampf um die Rechtswissenschaft"], was published in 1906 under the pseudonym "Gnaeus Flavius". The name of the Curulian aedile, who probably made a living as a scribe (*scriba pontificus*) in ancient Roman times, was well chosen. According to legend, in around 300 BC Gnaeus Flavius is credited with having made available to the general public the Roman clave formulas, which had been kept secret until then. More than two millennia later, Kantorowicz saw himself in the same role: he believed that he had to enlighten the public about the true reasons and motives that determine the application of law. His "Battle for Legal Science" is today considered one of the most important widely quoted legal writings of the twentieth century. On the very first page, the best-known manifesto of the Free Law Movement begins with an account of the finding of law by machines:

> The reigning ideal image of the jurist is as follows: higher civil servant with academic training, he sits in his cell, armed only with a thinking machine, certainly one of the finest kinds. The cell's only furnishing is a green table on which the State Code lies before him. Present him with any kind of situation, real or imaginary, and with the help of pure logical operations and a secret technique understood only by him, he is, as is demanded by his duty, able to deduce the decision in the legal code predetermined by the legislature with absolute precision.[6]

Here Kantorowicz creates the bizarre picture of a bureaucrat who, going against every aspect of reality, believes that he can extract the solution to every conceivable case from the law by means of a secret technique. The parallels to Jhering's "Judgment Machine" are unmistakable. Jhering also polemicized against the illusion of being able to see beforehand "the infinite variety and manifold formation of cases". He considered any attempt to limit the jurist to the law to be "misguided from the outset". The comparison

[6] Gnaeus Flavius, *Der Kampf um die Rechtswissenschaft* (1906), p. 7; Gnavius Flavius, "The Battle for Legal Science", transl. and annotated by Cory Merrill, *German Law Journal*, XII, no. 11, pp. 2006 -2030].

with the mechanical duck is intended to ridicule any and all efforts which aim to render "judicial thinking" superfluous by means of the mechanical application of the law.

When Jhering demonstrated the shortcomings of the application of the law with the aid of Vaucanson's famous automaton, the German Civil Code [Bürgerliches Gesetzbuch] was still under development. It came into effect on 1 January 1900, and therefore could not have been part of the cell's furnishings or have been placed on the table before the civil servant. This "green table" has been used ever since Kantorowicz created the memorable image as a metaphor for bureaucratic decisions made without reference to reality, real life, or practical considerations. Little has changed in this regard to this day, as can be seen in current German sports journalism, where people complain about the lack of connection to real life in the decision-making process, for example, when sports associations decide at the "green table" on a certain result after a soccer match has been called off. The only "furnishings" in the cell are the green table and the State Code. The machine itself is not present. The remoteness from everyday life is further emphasized by the fact that decisions are made in strict isolation, cut off from reality, in a cell. At least there is still a human being, a higher civil servant, making the decision. They have, however, been schooled, even "overbred", in such a way that their mind can only function as a machine. The decision generated by the machine lacks concreteness, individuality, active involvement, and transparency, and fails to include the circumstances of the case in question and "life". It is based on a secret technique, on "solely logical operations", that are understood, if at all, only by the person undertaking them. Considering the current discussion about legal tech, Kantorowicz's thinking machine is instructive for two reasons: first, because it hints at an analogy between mind and machine, and, second, because it touches on the problem of opacity. We shall return to both issues.

KANTOROWICZ AS THEORIST OF THE LEGAL MACHINE

From today's perspective, there is another reason that Kantorowicz's thinking machine deserves special attention with regard to legal tech: his "machine" opens a path to discussing problems from the viewpoints of legal philosophy and the theory of history that transcend an ordinary subsumption automaton or Jhering's "judgment machine". As already indicated, Jhering opposed a presumed jurisprudence of concepts, the formalism of which does not meet the requirements of everyday life and social reality. The doctrine of Free Law picked up on this critique directed primarily against Savigny and Puchta, but expanded on it in a twofold sense: first, it looks to the future, inasmuch as formalism also "infests" the new German Civil Code and, ultimately, all future law; and second, it looks to the past, via the science of pandects, back to the rational law of the seventeenth and eighteenth centuries, the Renaissance, the Middle Ages, and Antiquity. Kantorowicz in effect described a super-theory of the law in 1914, eight years after his "Battle for Legal Science", when he published an essay in "Die Tat", a magazine founded in 1909 and dedicated to cultural criticism. As the connections between the thinking machine and the "Epochs of Jurisprudence" [Die Epochen der Rechtswissenschaft (EdR)] have not yet been examined in depth, a brief description of the most important stages of Kantorowicz's "construction of history" is called for here.[7]

[7] Kantorowicz, EdR; see note 1 above. The guiding concepts to which Kantorowicz subjected jurisprudence were not new. Windscheid had characterized the history of jurisprudence as a pendulum swinging "between the formalistic application of law and the one that looks at the matter at hand". *Die Voraussetzung* (1892), in: *Gesammelte Reden und Abhandlungen*, ed. Paul Oertmann (1904), p. 408 et seq. Similarly, Savigny (see chapter 6) or Leibniz (see Stephan Meder, *Der unbekannte Leibniz* (2018), pp. 87-114) characterize the history of jurisprudence as an interplay between a stricter and a freer direction. Hans-Peter Haferkamp has recently objected that Kantorowicz has "tried to use legal history again as a source of meaning for the present": "Legal thought says something about legal thought. It says nothing about legal reality". See Haferkamp, "Lernen aus der Rechtsgeschichte? Hermann Kantorowicz und Friedrich Carl von Savigny", *JuristenZeitung*, LXXIV (2019), pp. 906, 909. It is true that Kantorowicz drew a skewed picture of legal history with his formalism narrative. However, historians are children of their time. They choose a certain topic and take a specific interest in it. What they look for, which questions they ask, or which answers they give depends on their place in the present. The fact that Kantorowicz has given an account of this deserves recognition. Appropriately, Nils Jansen stated, "Such accounts [of how it really had been – StM] increase the knowledge about the past, but without explanations they contribute little to the understanding of historical processes and social phenomena".

At the heart of the essay is a thesis that reduces the whole of jurisprudence to a conflict between two opposing forces or poles, which is ahistorical insofar as both are present at all times. The thesis states that the same opposition between "formalism" and "finalism" emerges "always anew" behind the façade of ever-changing forms and names (EdR, 1). Kantorowicz warns against overestimating the importance of these labels. Formalism and finalism are "nothing but catchwords" that easily lead one astray. Those who hesitate to use them can equally refer to rationalism and realism, positivism and verbalism, historicism and modernism, philological and teleological methods, or, "if they wish to sacrifice flexibility and definiteness of expression in favor of demotics, to a stricter and freer orientation" (EdR, 2). The crucial point is that the opposition between the poles always exists, as forms of thinking that are, as it were, situated beyond the law. What does this opposition consist of? First, Kantorowicz reminded us of two contrasting basic ideas that have remained in tension even until today. He pointed out that a distinction must be made between rules imposed by an authority standing above society, on the one hand, and, on the other, norms which grow independently of a sovereign will and from within society, as it were. Both positions are rooted in differing ideas about the origin of laws as either imposed by authorities through statutes, or formed on their own as a "spontaneous order". Jurists usually illustrate this difference with the division into written (*scriptum*) and unwritten (*non scriptum*) law, with the *ius scriptum* expressing the will of a national legislator and the *ius non scriptum* expressing the forces of society. In this context, it is understood that in the framework of *ius non scriptum*, judicial determination of law plays a unique role.

Hence, finalism puts more emphasis on the forces of society, whereas formalism gives greater deference to the legislator's mandate. The sphere to which finalism refers is reality, social reality, everyday life. The basis for formalism, on the other hand, is the legal text – the "official code of law", a weapon in the hands of a "senior civil servant". Formalistic

Nils Jansen, "Der Gegenstand der Rechtswissenschaft", *JuristenZeitung*, LXXV (2020), pp. 219.

legal thinking thus harmonizes with the idea of an authority standing above society constructing a closed system of theorems and concepts, from which the knowledge of the law is then derived with almost mechanical consistency. Finalism, on the other hand, takes reality as its starting point and seeks to give an answer to the purposes, interests, and demands of life. Kantorowicz enumerated a range of further conceptual contradictions that result from the difference between formalism and finalism, opining that the character of the "formalist orientations" will be more

> verbalistic, theoretical, passive, receptive, and conservative, while the character of the finalistic orientation will be more realistic, practical, critical, productive, and progressive. The former will gladly turn its gaze to the past and strive to keep it alive in the present, the latter will look at the present and seek to pave the way for aspirations pointing to a vigorous future. (EdR, 2)

Kantorowicz considered that both orientations, that is, formalism as well as finalism, remain present "at all times". How is this proclamation to be understood? Does every epoch of jurisprudence contain both elements at the same time? The question must be answered in the negative, although Kantorowicz was indeed sometimes understood to mean that. In fact, he wants to say that the two forms appear in each instance in a "pure" sense, in the form of an either/or, so that in the epochs of jurisprudence "now the one, now the other prevailed" (EdR, 2). By assuming a categorical difference, the tension between the two forms of thought is not only intensified but is virtually absolutized in the sense of an all-or-nothing. Against this background, it seems only logical that Kantorowicz longs for a victory of finalism over formalism:

> One was formalistic: whoever wanted to write a book [...] put together the most varied discussions on the basis of external points of view [...] One split hairs: loved useless disputes and distinctions [...] One was pedantic: carried out the mentioned forms of reasoning schematically, even where they became unsuitable [...] One was above all blind and faithful to authority [...]

> We have here [...] the full-blown historicism, living outside its own time, and accordingly an almost complete lack of historical sense before us. Life went its way, and science went its. (EdR, 4 et seq.)

These claims are directed against the Glossators who initiated the reception of Roman law in Bologna towards the end of the eleventh century. At their "gateway" stood "a formal, philological achievement": "the discovery of several ancient books, the improvement of their text from other ancient books" (EdR, 4). Strictly speaking, however, Kantorowicz's outline of formalism in the Epochs of Jurisprudence began much earlier: with Justinian and his order for the compilation of the *Corpus Iuris* in Byzantium in the first half of the sixth century. In our context, it is worth emphasizing that even at this early stage there is talk of the machine-like and the mechanical nature of law-abiding application of the law. Justinian's demands that legislation be complete and coherent, and be rigidly bound to the texts, had stood in the way of dealing with the law more freely. Justinian had

> forbidden any treatment of the sources beyond the mechanical, especially of their main body, the Digest, under the penalty of that which befalls the forger. In these words of the Byzantine emperor - not as is often taught, in the authoritative dogma of the Middle Ages - lies the historical root of the subsequent conception of jurisprudence as the 'handmaiden' of the legislator (EdR, 4 et seq.)

With Justinian, "we see for the first time" that the "jurist should be the mindless tool of the legislator". And from the eleventh century onwards, in the reception of Roman law, "this doctrine dominated the study of law in mainland Europe":[8]

[8] Both citations: Kantorowicz, *Aus der Vorgeschichte der Freirechtslehre* (1925), in Kantorowicz, *Rechtswissenschaft und Soziologie: Ausgewählte Schriften zur Wissenschaftslehre,* ed. Thomas Würtenberger (1962), pp. 48, 49. For the connection of tool and machine, see chapter 5, notes 12 und 13.

> The whole reception of Roman law in Germany can therefore be understood as a process within the 'jurisprudence of concepts', that aberration of legal thought which constructs its concepts without practical consideration of the practical consequences, or adopts them from somewhere and then applies them to circumstances, however individual they may be. (EdR, 8)

From the Glossators runs a line through the Postglossators, the Humanist Jurists, the Law of Reason, and on to the Historical School of Savigny and Puchta. But the question remains: can an epoch be found in which finalism reigned supreme? Kantorowicz would probably draw a clear distinction here between classical Roman jurisprudence and a direction that became influential in the second half of the nineteenth century. The Romans, at least at their best, were "practitioners of the purest sort": They were "tainted not at all by historicism, and little by the jurisprudence of concepts". They deserve credit for supplementing the incomplete formal law "with free law".[9] Interpretation and equity played a decisive role in this context. The particular merit of classical Roman jurisprudence was that it placed "equity" (*aequitas*) entirely at the center of the application of law. It is true that the Romans often decided according to "feeling" and were hardly able to give reasons for their reference to equity. Nevertheless, their decisions were usually "on the mark", for their sense of justice had been "trained" by observing the requirements of everyday life and had been refined into a kind of "emotional jurisprudence". Thus, they were able to "identify the means of law that serve to satisfy these requirements".[10] Only in the second half of the nineteenth century would there be increasing signs that a "realist" direction was "gradually regaining the upper hand".

Kantorowicz is here referring to the "Younger School of the History of Law" which, after Jhering, "still holds sway today" (EdR, 13). This Younger School, of course,

[9] Kantorowicz, note 8 above, pp. 46, 45.

[10] Ibid., p. 46.

could only be understood "as a mixture of formalist and finalist elements" (EdR, 13). The reason for this "mixture" is due to the Historical School of Law's dual concern with legal construction and practical jurisprudence, in which formalistic and finalistic elements are readily confused.

It is precisely here, however, that the analytical dimension of the historical construction established in the essay substantiates itself: the formalist narrative helps to separate and isolate the two elements from each other in such a way that even the smallest remnant of formalism can be identified and discarded. These remarks indicate that Kantorowicz understood this "mixture" as a contradiction that demands resolution (EdR, 13 et seq.) From this side, too, it is evident that he believed he must draw a categorical line of distinction between formalism and finalism. With impressive consistency, Kantorowicz pursued an unchanging goal: the victory of finalism, which can only be celebrated when even the smallest remnant of formalism had been eradicated.

FORMALISM AS STRONGHOLD AGAINST ARBITRARY EXERCISE OF STATE POWER AND KADI JUSTICE?

How should this approach be evaluated? The rigorous rejection of formalism played, albeit unintentionally, into the hands of National Socialist jurists who had a completely different and previously unknown interest in discrediting the accomplishments of the nineteenth century: under the banner of "anti-formalism", their aim was to help a new "ideology" to prevail with as little hindrance as possible. History taught them that, after relinquishing its attachment to formal law, jurisprudence would be at the mercy of assaults from politics, ethics, or values. Numerous historical examples bear witness to the dire consequences of how the principle of abstract equality was dispensed during the National Socialist era or how the legal practice of expropriation was applied, where formal legal positions were invalidated by the assertion of a heteronomously determined "national spirit". The terminology was partly preempted by the doctrine of Free Law. For example, Kantorowicz suggested that, instead of following the "jurisprudence of letters and concepts", a judge should choose the "*sociological path*", stating: "However, it is to be taken into account that in this case a sound, popular, not 'unworldly' feeling and a sound mind are more important than theoretical knowledge: Not everything that can be *learned* and must be *learned*, needs to be or can be *taught* in the form of an academic subject".[11] Kantorowicz could not have foreseen that the academic regulations for law courses introduced by the Nazis in 1935, some twenty years later, would seek to cultivate a new type of lawyer who was no longer a "bookworm" and who, before sitting for the professorial legal qualification examination for example, was to stay in a camp with compulsory flag-saluting in the morning and field exercises.[12]

[11] Kantorowicz, note 2 above, p. 127 (emphasis in the original). See also Fuchs, *Gefühlsjurisprudenz* (1912), in: *Gesammelte Schriften,* note 3 above, p. 67. That Kantorowicz understood the tension between formalism and finalism in the sense of either/or and that he sought to eliminate formalism, can be seen in the assumption that jurisdiction had lost its characteristic predictability and uniformity, and in the assertion that ideals of legality, reasonableness, academic conditions, and legal certainty could not be achieved. See *Der Kampf um die Rechtswissenschaft,* note 6 above, p. 29 et seq. This is not contradicted by his occasionally emphasizing that he did not want to advocate liberating the courts from being bound by the laws. *Rechtswissenschaft und Soziologie,* note 2 above, p. 124 et seq. Kantorowicz never felt it necessary to state anywhere whether and how formal law could resist the excesses of total finalization (or materialization) in the event of a conflict, so this seems to be little more than paying lip service. In any case, an independent character cannot be attributed to this 'commitment' to finalism.

[12] In more detail, Stephan Meder, *Rechtsgeschichte* (6th ed.; 2017), pp. 415-421, 426. The Heidelberg lecturer Heinz Hildebrandt, for example, reported on such camp life in the introduction to a hitherto little-noticed work on "Rechtsfindung im neuen deutschen Staate" (1935), which revolves around "jurisprudence of concepts" following the doctrine of Free Law. As a radical critic of formalism and National Socialist jurist, Hildebrandt summarized his "highest guiding principle" as follows: "*It is not the concept that should determine life, but life that should determine the concept*" (p. 93 – emphasis in the orignal). Thus, it is in the sign of "life" that the traditional legal order is to be destroyed and a "limitless interpretation" (Bernd Rüthers, 1968) is to be legitimized. This conclusion, however, must not obscure the fact that interpretation in Nazi jurisprudence was also strongly "limited" or reduced to zero, namely by the Führer's will, as Hildebrandt also points out. In truth, the "supreme guiding principle" should have been: "Not the concept should determine the Führer's will, but the Führer's will should determine the concept". Such a formula, of course, could never have been agreed to by the jurists of the Free Law Movement with their more "left-wing" political convictions directed against the legal establishment. The term

After the Second World War, parts of academia, opposed to the doctrine of free law or Nazi jurisprudence, tended again to favor formal law as the experience of the chaotic consequences of totalitarian rule created the conditions for a renewed appreciation of the value of reliable forms for securing freedom and justice within a democratic society. One problem with Kantorowicz's narrative is that formalism also existed before the emergence of classical Roman jurisprudence, namely in the ancient Roman period. However, this formalism had nothing to do with theory, system, or academia, nor with a lack of practical experience, but was due to the orality of ancient Roman legal culture.[13] Kantorowicz had failed to recognize that there existed a formalism which sprang directly from the experiences of "everyday life". This also applies *mutatis mutandis* to modern formalism insofar as social values are expressed in it and it is to be understood as a stronghold against governmental arbitrariness and kadi justice.

The "historical construction" created over the epochs of jurisprudence is a history of decline, which begins with the fall of Roman law in the post-classical epoch, continues through the epochs of the Middle Ages, the law of reason, and Pandectics, and persists until today. Although the doctrine of Free Law and its finalist method may appear as a kind of light at the end of a millennia-long tunnel, the dangers in this orientation are undeniable. They lie "in the fate of its scholastic and rationalist predecessors" (EdR, 14). Thus, it is only a matter of time before jurisprudence returns to formalism, until a renewed construction and closedness of concepts displace its life-related elements. Kantorowicz suspected that the doctrine of Free Law, should it ever come to dominate, would remain only an episode.

KANTOROWICZ'S "CONSTRUCTION OF HISTORY" IN A CONTEMPORARY CONTEXT

"unlimited interpretation" thus captures only a partial aspect and is hardly suitable for defining what should constitute National Socialist jurisprudence (for discussions and references, not least to Hildebrandt's monograph, I thank Andrea Czelk).

[13] Meder, note 12 above, pp. 55-72.

Concepts such as reality, life, Being, or Existence were still in vogue after 1914 and in the 1920s and 1930s reached a peak of cultural-philosophical relevance that has probably never been repeated. Martin Heidegger, Gottfried Benn, Hans Freyer, and Friedrich Gundolf are often referred to as examples of authors whose thinking revolved around a negative demarcation of rationalism, intellectualism, scientism, and a "new reality".[14] The basis for this was an intellectual current that emerged in the second half of the nineteenth century and was called "philosophy of life" after such different authors as Wilhelm Dilthey, Friedrich Nietzsche, or Henri Bergson. It was intended as a counterproposal to positivism and neo-Kantianism, which were accused of one-sidedly emphasizing rationality in the manner of the natural sciences. The starting point of the philosophy of life is the concrete experience of the individual human being, whose wholeness cannot be grasped by conceptual constructions or logic alone. The view that an encompassing life comprises creative, non-rational, dynamic elements and – in addition to reason – feelings, intuitions, instincts, or impulses was above all the view of Oswald Spengler (1880-1936), doctor of philosophy, and erstwhile schoolteacher.

Oswald Spengler and the Decline of the Occident

Only three years after Kantorowicz's Epochs of Legal History, in 1917, Spengler examined more closely the relationship between law and reality in his main work on the philosophy of culture, the bestseller on the "Decline of the West" [Untergang des Abendlandes, (UdA)], which is being revisited today. The parallels with Kantorowicz's narrative of formalism are striking: Spengler characterized jurists as "slaves of concepts", whereas "*private law is to represent the spirit of respective social and economic existences*".[15] He also

[14] Otto Gerhard Oexle, "„Wirklichkeit" – „Krise der Wirklichkeit" – „Neue Wirklichkeit". Deutungsmuster und Paradigmenkämpfe in der deutschen Wissenschaft vor und nach 1933", in Frank-Rutger Hausmann (ed.), *Die Rolle der Geisteswissenschaften im Dritten Reich 1933-1945* (2002), pp. 1-20 (see also the "highest guiding principle" in note 12 above).

[15] Oswald Spengler, *Der Untergang des Abendlandes. Umrisse einer Morphologie der Weltgeschichte* (1917), Beck'sche Sonderausgabe (1981),

regarded classical Roman law with its free determination of law by the praetor as an ideal, a model, and an example unsurpassed to this day:

> The judge as a rank, trained expertly and even theoretically for carrying out this activity, is quite unknown in Antiquity [...]. The Romans were not systematists nor historians nor theoreticians in this respect, but merely brilliant practitioners. Their jurisprudence is empirical scholarship of individual cases, a technique penetrated by cerebral analysis, not a building of abstractions. (UdA, 625 et seq.)

For Spengler, Byzantium, scholasticism, rational law, and Pandectics were the stages that led to the "celebrated 'petrification of the official law'" – the "true symbol of a late civilization" (UdA, 633). The legal history of the West begins with "Germanic tribal rights", which were soon superseded by the "creation of Justinian": The "utter insignificance" of this creation is attested "by the fact that the main part, the Pandects, was preserved in a single manuscript, which was found by chance – unfortunately – in around 1050" (UdA, 644). After that date, the judges "north of the Alps were obliged to study and they received their experience, not from the life that surrounded them but from a concept-splitting philology" (UdA, 646). From here, it is only a small step to the general "mechanization of the world" that Spengler deplored a few years later in his work on "Man and Technology" [Mensch und Technik], which has been reprinted many times. These few notes and excerpts suffice to give a first impression of the connections between Kantorowicz's narrative of formalism and a philosophy of life as a story of decline.

Fritz Pringsheim's Critique of the "Mechanical" Apparatus

An evaluation of the history of jurisprudence as a history of decline can also be found in the work of Fritz Pringsheim

p. 650 – hereinafter cited as UdA (emphasis in the original); see also: Lutz Martin Keppeler, *Oswald Spengler und die Jurisprudenz* (2014), for example, p. 86.

(1882-1967), teacher of Franz Wieacker, to whose narrative of formalism we will return shortly. In his famous essay "Beryt und Bologna" (1921), Pringsheim, who was familiar with Kantorowicz's Epochs of Jurisprudence, also favored early classical Roman jurisprudence: "In a very peculiar way, theory and practice were intertwined here"; "everything was in complete movement".[16] By contrast, Byzantium and the Justinian codification are met with radical rejection. The first signs of the decline and fracture completed during the Byzantine epoch had become visible in 117 CE, that is, with Hadrian, when a "body of bureaucrats was formed after the model of the Hellenistic monarchies". There arose "an officially organized body, an officiating structure", which "obeyed fixed rules" and worked with "machine-like precision." The consequences for jurists were serious. Pringsheim described them:

> The apparatus can tolerate only colorless specialists. They are produced by a legal professional training. It has been said that the post-classical jurists were all extremely mediocre, although in that period there were both schools and teachers. The opposite is true. *Because* the lawyers are no good, there must be both schools and teachers.17

As with Kantorowicz or Spengler, Pringsheim demonstrated the antagonism between theory and practice, between norms and case law, between rigidity and motion,

[16] Pringsheim differentiated between "scholarly jurisprudence" and "practical direction": "The distinction touches upon that between formalist and finalist directions in Kantorowicz's *Die Epochen der Rechtswissenschaft*". See Pringsheim, *Beryt und Bologna* (1921), in: id, *Gesammelte Abhandlungen* (1961), I, p. 392. On the exemplarity of Roman jurists and their "falling silent": *Höhe und Ende der römischen Jurisprudenz* (1933), in ibid., pp. 55, 61. See Viktor Winkler, *Der Kampf gegen die Rechtswissenschaft* (2014), p. 90.

[17] Quoted from Pringsheim, note 16 above, p. 56 (onset of decline already with Hadrian) [Einsetzen des Verfalls schon mit Hadrian], p. 59 (bureaucracy as machine) [Bürokratie als Maschine]. On the decline caused by Byzantium and the Justinian Codification: Pringsheim, *Die archaistische Tendenz Justinians* (1929), in: id, *Gesammelte Abhandlungen* (1961), II, p. 10 ("the longing for the simplicity and primitiveness of the early times" as the "hallmark of the consummating decay") ["die Sehnsucht nach der Einfachheit und Primitivität der frühen Zeiten" als das "Kennzeichen des sich vollendenden Verfalles"].

between academic theory and empirical study, between system and life, to name but a few examples. Closer examination, however, also reveals differences, which can only be touched upon briefly here. Pringsheim did not sharpen the differences between the two forms of thought in such a way that they appear as either/or. Thus, in the ideal state of early classical Roman law, there did not yet exist a "legal doctrine that proceeded on the basis of theory". This does not mean that there was no theory in this early state of law, however: "In a rather unique way, theory and practice were intertwined here". Indeed, there was "reliance on a rule once it had been established". "The rule and equitable adaptation to the particularities of the individual case struggled with each other", and were consequently in a state of constant interaction.[18] Unlike Kantorowicz and later Wieacker, Pringsheim thus considered it entirely desirable that law – at least within a certain framework – be predetermined on the basis of solid and constant forms.

CONSEQUENCES TO THE PRESENT DAY? FRANZ WIEACKER AND THE 'MATERIALIZATION THESIS'

The differentiation between formal and material law is among the widely debated topics in the fields of theory, history, and dogmatics of private law. Throughout, the starting point is Franz Wieacker's (1908-1994) observation that jurisprudence under the aegis of the Reichsgericht has "transformed the formal ethic of freedom that underpinned the German private law system *back* into a material ethic of social responsibility".[19] This phrase shows: Wieacker, who

[18] Quotations from Pringsheim, note 16 above, p. 55.

[19] Wieacker, *Das Sozialmodell der klassischen Privatrechtsgesetzbücher und die Entwicklung der modernen Gesellschaft* (1953), in: id, *Industriegesellschaft und Privatrechtsordnung* (1974), p. 24. For the current discussion, see the references in Claus-Wilhelm Canaris, "Wandlungen des Schuldvertragsrechts – Tendenzen zu seiner Materialisierung", *Archiv für die civilistische Praxis*, CC (2000), pp. 273-364; Gerhard Wagner, "Materialisierung des Schuldrechts unter dem Einfluss von Verfassungsrecht und Europarecht", in Uwe Blaurock and Günter Hager (eds.), *Obligationenrecht im 21. Jahrhundert* (2010), pp. 13-84; Günter Hager, *Strukturen des Privatrechts in Europa* (2012), pp. 3-23; Marietta Auer, *Der privatrechtliche Diskurs der Moderne* (2014). Wieacker considered Kantorowicz's formalism narrative with its classification of

was equally well acquainted with Kantorowicz's types of scientific thought, only takes on "formalism", but not "finalism".

Instead of "final", he chooses "material" – a term found in nineteenth century jurisprudence, for instance in the works of Bernhard Windscheid or Gottlieb Planck, but which only gained prominence through the worldwide success of Max Weber's sociology of law. Max Weber, whose differentiation between formal and material rationality will be the subject of the next chapter, described the classical model of law as "formal" in the sense that "exclusively unambiguous general elements of statutory definition are considered" in the finding of the law. In contrast, it would be possible to have recourse, under the premises of "material" law, to legal principles that originated in the fields of politics or ethics beyond the elements of statutory definition. Wieacker thought that jurisprudence had to transform the formal ethics of freedom of the Historical School of Law back into a material ethics of social responsibility because the juridical formalism dominant in the nineteenth century had not been able to meet the needs of everyday legal practice.

In agreement with Kantorowicz, Wieacker thus understood formalism as a concept of conflict that must be juxtaposed against the teachings of Savigny and Puchta: Savigny's jurisprudential positivism "emerged from the formalism of Kant's critique of knowledge" and would therefore be "much more aptly described as jurisprudential *formalism*".[20] Denial of the "social purpose", disregard for "social justice," and distance from "life" are characteristics that Wieacker believed he must ascribe to the Historical School of Law. The concern of the "materialization thesis", then, is to correct these shortcomings. What does this mean for formal law? Should it be completely abandoned in order to declare "life", practical considerations, the specific facts of an individual case, to be the measure of all things? Kantorowicz, who, as indicated, aimed at a complete

thought forms to be an "ingenious attempt at intellectual-historical style characterization", *Privatrechtsgeschichte der Neuzeit* (2nd ed.; 1967), p. 20, at note 19.

[20] Wieacker, note 19 above, p. 432.

eradication of legal formalism, would indeed have drawn this consequence. Is the same true for Wieacker? The question must be asked because his "materialization thesis" still has many supporters.

In 1977, the Italian legal historian and editor of the *Quaderni Fiorentini*, Paolo Grossi, asked Wieacker how he viewed his critique of jurisprudential formalism, which had essentially been worked out in the 1930s. Wieacker replied that, although he now viewed many aspects in a different light, he still did not believe that formal law could be used to build a "bulwark of civil liberties".[21] This deserves to be emphasized because Wieacker's historical narrative is also based on those same coordinates that Kantorowicz differentiated in his "ingenious attempt at intellectual-historical stylistic characterization".[22] Formalism, he argued, can be traced from post-classical Roman law and the Byzantine era through Justinian's *Corpus iuris*, the reception of Roman law in the Middle Ages, the law of reason, and Pandectics all the way to the contemporary law of the day. Wieacker, too, believed that reality has its own immanent justice which finds direct expression in the decision-making practice of jurists. In particular, early classical Roman jurisprudence had achieved the ideal of such a practice completely disconnected from theory. In contrast, he stated, the systems created by the Byzantines, glossators, rational jurists, or pandectists were excesses of an unprecedented history of decay.[23]

Rights cannot be prescribed by dependable forms of securing freedom and justice. Just as Kantorowicz, Wieacker

[21] Wieacker, "‚Wandlungen der Eigentumsverfassung' revisited", *Quaderni Fiorentini 5–6: Itinerari moderni della proprietá* (1976–77), II, pp. 841-843. On this view also Okko Behrends, "Nachruf Wieacker", *Zeitschrift der Savigny-Stiftung für Rechtsgeschichte (Romanistische Abteilung)*, CXII (1995), pp. xxxvii, xxx.

[22] Thus, the aforementioned formulation by Wieacker, note 19 above, p. 20 (it should be noted that Kantorowicz, in retrospect, considered the epoch essay itself to be his most important work).

[23] References in Stephan Meder, "Franz Wieackers 'Wandlungen im Bilde der historischen Rechtsschule' neu gelesen: Ein schiefes Bild der Rechtsgeschichte?", in: *FS für Albert Janssen* (to be published). On this in more detail, see Behrends, note 21 above, pp. xiiii-lxii. See also Winkler, note 16 above, pp. 370-377.

argued that formal law must be dissolved because justice can only be found in judgements, only in the practical setting, only in the immanence of the decision-making situation. These are the positions of the free finding of the law, which, admittedly unconsciously, still survive in the "materialization thesis".

As far as is apparent, Wieacker did not explicitly refer to the image of the "thinking machine". In an early paper from 1938, however, he rejected the idea that the "German judge" had ever been a "subsumption automaton".[24] Almost thirty years later, Wieacker returned to the subject of legal machines under quite different circumstances: The "subsumption automaton" represented an image of judges that is "in some way reminiscent of the programmed electronic computers of the present day".[25] In effect, the historian displayed an interest in the still young discipline of legal informatics, which has subsequently intensified with several contributions on automatic decision-making.[26] Ultimately, Wieacker warns against overestimating the technological achievements of binary systems, because "in legal matters there are usually no apodictic decisions of truth versus untruth, but rather also solutions that are 'more correct' or 'more incorrect'". This was the reason why the various currents within legal studies had paid so much attention to the open and movable parts of jurisprudence. As examples, Wieacker referred to the doctrine of Free Law, but, what may be surprising, also to Puchta.[27] Apparently, he did have an idea of the extent to

[24] Wieacker, "Richtermacht und privates Rechtsverhältnis. Eine Übersicht zum Stand der Problematik im Privatrecht", *Archiv des öffentlichen Rechts,* LXVIII (1938), p. 2. In the background is apparently Wieacker's appreciation of "German supreme court jurisprudence in the second half of the 19th century". See "Rechtsgewinnung durch elektronische Datenverarbeitung?", in: *Festschrift für Ernst v. Caemmerer* (1978), p. 60 and p. 50 (for discussions and references to this contribution thanks are expressed to Wolfgang Kilian).

[25] Wieacker, note 19 above, p. 436.

[26] See for example Wieacker, "Recht und Automation", in: *Festschrift für Eduard Bötticher zum 70. Geburtstag* (1969), pp. 383-404; Wieacker (1978), note 24 above. On the beginnings of legal informatics, see also chapter 8 below.

[27] Wieacker, note 26 above, p. 400. The fact that a legal machine requires a considerable level of "schematization", that its programming requires

which Puchta, using notions of equity and interpretation, allowed material elements to enter into the framework of his system. Only the name Savigny is missing, which seems only consistent in view of the alleged reliance on Kant's "critique of knowledge formalism".

"the specification of binary decision patterns according to a finite set of clearly defined rigid criteria", is still seen as a problem in current literature. See for example Frederik v. Harbou, "Abschied vom Einzelfall? – Perspektiven der Digitalisierung von Verwaltungsverfahren", *JuristenZeitung*, LXXV (2020), p. 346 (for details, see chapters 8 and 9 below).

Chapter 3
Max Weber:
Transformation of the Judge into an Automaton of Paragraphs and Precedents

Max Weber (1864-1920) is known in academic circles primarily as a sociologist and national economist, and less as a jurist and legal historian. However, his work contains multi-layered reflections on the formalization of the application of the law with a remarkable degree of correspondence to Kantorowicz's "Epochen der Rechtswissenschaft". In a little-noticed study on "Roman and German Law" [Römisches und deutsches Recht] (1895), published at the same time as the German Civil Code [Bürgerliches Gesetzbuch] was being compiled, Weber considered the "increasing capacity of jurists to think exclusively formally" to be a problem. He stated that legal formalism, while containing "indispensable advances", had also led to an estrangement from society. The consequence, he said, was that civil law no longer had any "directly tangible meaning" for the individual. The excesses of formalism and rationalism brought jurisdiction into a position

> in which the necessity that men and not machines sit on the bench appears to be but a regrettable imperfection. The ideal of this understanding would be the transformation of the judge into an automaton of paragraphs and precedents, into whose top the facts and the costs are thrown, so that he can spew out the verdict together with the reasoning at the bottom.1

1 Max Weber, "'Römisches' und 'deutsches' Recht" (1895), *Christliche Welt*, IX (1895), pp. 521-525. Also in *Max Weber-Gesamtausgabe, Abteilung I: Landarbeiterfrage, Nationalstaat und Volkswirtschaftspolitik. Schriften und Reden 1892-1899*, IV(1) (1993), p. 533 et seq. (hereinafter: MWG I/4-1).

From the viewpoint of the courts, nothing would be more alarming "than if they were put in the position of having to *evaluate* phenomena from the socio-political or socio-ethical point of view". The "broad average mass of contemporary jurists" would lack the prerequisites "to fill a greater and more dignified role". And in his "Sociology of Law" [Rechtssoziologie], written nearly a decade later (1914) and published posthumously (1922), Weber once again posed the question: what would happen if one were to take away from judges "their belief in the sanctity of purely objective legal formalism and [were to] direct them simply to balance interests?"[2]

Modern law has apparently fallen into a "crisis" which manifests itself in excessive formalism and rationalism. Looked at in this light, the desire for machines rather than humans to be "seated on the judge's chair" in the future can only seem rational. There is, however, another side of the coin; namely, the radical demand for complete dissolution of legal formalism: Would not it be better for laypersons to be "seated on the bench"? Do not abstract general concepts, the system, the logic, the scholarship, and university education obscure the view of what actually matters: social reality and social justice – reality and everyday life? Questions of this nature began to be raised by the protagonists of antiformal movements after around 1900. Weber tried to explain how anti-formalism was able to gain such a rapidly growing group of followers in such a short time:

> Being confined to the interpretation of statutes and contracts, like a slot machine into which one just drops the facts (plus the fee) in order to have it spew out the decision (plus opinion), appears to the modern lawyer as beneath his dignity; and the more universal the codified formal statute law has become, the more

[2] Max Weber, *Rechtssoziologie* (1922), in: Weber, *Wirtschaft und Gesellschaft. Grundriß der verstehenden Soziologie*, ed. Johannes Winckelmann (5th ed.; 1985), pp. 512 (hereinafter cited as WuG); reprinted in *Max Weber-Gesamtausgabe, Abteilung I: Schriften und Reden*, XXII(3) (2010), pp. 274-639, MWG I/22-3). All English translations taken from: Max Weber, *Economy and Society. An Outline of Interpretive Sociology*, eds. Guenther Roth and Claus Wittich (reprint.; 2007).

unattractive has this notion come to be. The present demand is for judicial "creativeness".[3]

The anti-formalists have thus chosen the judge-king as their model. Weber interpreted the ever-increasing demand for a "creative" jurisprudence as a consequence of excessive formalism and rationalism, as a result of the "continuous growth of formal statute law and, especially, of systematic codification". Not least, then, in the shadow of the freshly implemented Civil Code, the "academic scholars" felt "themselves to be painfully threatened both in their importance and in their opportunities for unencumbered intellectual activity" (WuG, 509). Weber alluded here both to the year 1900 and to the fact that immediately after its entry into force, jurists supplemented, corrected, and modified the BGB to an astonishing extent "not only *praeter legem* but also *contra legem*". As early as 1905, the German Reichsgericht

[3] *Rechtssoziologie* (WuG), p. 507. It has been claimed that terms such as legal automaton, judgment machine, or subsumption machine are generally pejorative. Weber's formulation is "irritating" because it suggests that there was a time when mechanical certainty in the field of legal application was considered a necessity or even desirable. See Clara Günzl, "Subsumtionsautomaten und -maschinen. Rechtshistorische Anmerkungen zu einem beliebten Vorwurf", *JuristenZeitung*, LXXIV (2019), p. 181. Unlike Jhering, Kantorowicz, and many other authors, Weber certainly did not have in mind here the putative jurisprudence of concepts in the first half of the nineteenth century (he did not use the term "Begriffsjurisprudenz", and he considered Jhering's theses to be outdated in their essential aspects). This does not mean, however, that such a period did not exist, as will be discussed in chapter 6 below. Moreover, there are many passages in Weber's work in which the machine metaphor does play an important role, but they cannot all be listed here (see note 13 below). It should only be noted that Weber associated the machine with not only legal decision-making, but also with the more general phenomenon of increasing bureaucratization in social life: "An inanimate machine is mind objectified. Only this provides it with the power to force men into its service [...] Objectified intelligence is also that animated machine, the bureaucratic organization, with its specialization of trained skills, its division of jurisdiction, its rule and hierarchical relations of authority". *Soziologie der Herrschaft*, in WuG, note 2 above, p. 835). "The fully developed bureaucratic apparatus compares with other organizations exactly as does the machine with the non-mechanical modes of production. Precision, speed, unambiguity, knowledge of the files, continuity, discretion, unity, strict subordination, reduction of friction and of material and personal costs — these are raised to the optimum point in the strictly bureaucratic administration, and especially in its monocratic form. As compared with all collegiate, honorific, and avocational forms of administration, trained bureaucracy is superior on all". Ibid., p. 651.

pronounced the momentous principle that a decision in the field of civil law need not be derived from the paragraphs of the Civil Code in every case.[4] The "doctrine of Free Law" therefore had undertaken to prove,

> that such silence is the inevitable fate of every statute in view of the irrationality of the facts of life; that in countless instances the application of the statutes as "interpreted" is a delusion, and that the decision is, and ought to be, made in the light of concrete evaluations rather than in accordance with formal norms. (WuG, 507)

The creative activity of the Reichsgericht thus proves once again: jurisprudence cannot be determined by preset laws. Instead, it is a free finding of law, which at the same time suggested the superiority of English law with its use of precedents. In view of the one-sidedness of formalism, Weber certainly did not intend to deny that these theses at the heart of the doctrine of Free Law have a certain plausibility. He also stated that the German Civil Code sometimes veered too strongly in the direction of formalism, citing the phrase "Kauf bricht Miete" (a lease is terminated by the sale of the land), adopted from Antiquity by the drafters of the German Civil Code, as an example of drafting "entirely due to a blind desire for logical consistency" (WuG, 459). On the other hand, scholars of the doctrine of Free Law strained logic in the other direction. Weber stated that they lacked historical understanding for the additions and amendments by the Reichsgericht, which were to be understood merely as the symptom of a temporary accommodation by the jurists of the constraints of *ius scriptum*. Weber did not criticize the Free Law Movement anywhere directly. He even attested

[4] "Urteil des Reichsgerichts vom 28. Januar 1905", *Entscheidungen des Reichsgerichts in Zivilsachen*, LX, p. 58 et seq. (although the authors of the BGB would not have included the *clausula rebus sic stantibus* in the Code, from the point of view of equity the changed circumstances "in the individual case" could nevertheless be taken into account; why this is so and must be so was fastidiously explained by the Reichsgericht) [zwar hätten die Verfasser des BGB die *clausula rebus sic stantibus* nicht in das Gesetzbuch aufgenommen, unter dem Gesichtspunkt der Billigkeit könne den veränderten Umständen „im einzelnen Falle" aber gleichwohl Rechnung getragen werden; warum dem so ist und so sein muss, hat das Reichsgericht anspruchsvoll begründet].

that it "undoubtedly attracts the best minds today", and worked hard to ensure that Hermann Kantorowicz spoke at the First Conference of the German Society for Sociology (1910).[5] However, between the extremes of legal automatism and judge kingship, Weber's critique of the doctrine of Free Law can be pieced together quite clearly.

HOW EXTENSIVE ARE THE SIMILARITIES WITH KANTOROWICZ'S FORMALISM NARRATIVE?

At first glance, there seems to be a close relationship between Kantorowicz's "Epochen der Rechtswissenschaft" and that concurrent history of knowledge that is expressed in Weber's "Sociology of Law". Weber also differentiates between two contrasting types of legal thinking, the practical and the theoretical type. A "fairly pure illustration" of the practical type is the guild-like English method of legal training – an empirical method that does not entail subsumption or syllogism. In Weber's view, in this type "one always moves from the particular to the particular but never tries to move from the particular to general propositions in order to be able subsequently to deduce from them norms for new particular cases": "No rational legal training or theory can ever arise in such a situation."

The second type of legal thinking – the theoretical – deals with "general concepts". These are formed "by abstraction from concreteness or by logical interpretation of meaning, or by generalization and subsumption, and are used in syllogistically applicable norms".[6] There is therefore a parallel with Kantorowicz in the way Weber also linked the contrasts to their respective social agents by contrasting the training of practitioners with academic teaching. Weber considered university teaching to be the nucleus of any rational legal system and, with the reception of Roman law, this type of legal thinking has been carried through to the present via glossators and commentators. Along with Kantorowicz, Weber believed that the groundwork was laid in Byzantium. The scholarly work cultivated there had an

[5] Max Weber, "Brief an Hermann Beck v. 12. September 1910", in: *Max Weber-Gesamtausgabe, Abteilung II: Briefe* (1994), VI, p. 607 (MWG II/6).

[6] All citations from *Rechtssoziologie* (WuG), pp. 465, 457, 458.

impact that can still be felt today, at least on the European continent. In "Sociology of Law", Weber wrote that Roman legal life

> lacked not only a synthetic-constructive but also a rational-systematic character, and it did so much more than has at times been assumed. It was the Byzantine bureaucracy which finally systematized the existing law; but as far as the formal rigor of juridical thought was concerned, it stood far behind the achievements of the jurisconsults of the Republic and the Principate. (WuG, 464 et seq.)

Notwithstanding all the similarities, this statement reveals a first difference: Kantorowicz saw the merit of (early) classical Roman jurisprudence in the freedom of legal finding – in finalism, which works against any "formal rigor" and seeks to dissolve it in the end. Weber sees its "purely formal aspects" as a particular achievement of classical jurisprudence, as the "most important aspects from a general historical point of view" of Roman law (WuG, 463). How can this contrast be explained? First, let us recall Kantorowicz's warning against overvaluing terminology: the term "rationalism" is entirely suitable for describing formalism. For Kantorowicz, then, formalism and rationalism mean roughly the same thing; both have a negative connotation. From Weber's point of view, however, formal legal thinking should be the motor for rationalization, for "predictability" in law as a characteristic of modern culture. Thus, while Weber saw "formalism" as an indispensable feature of legal progress, he managed without the term "finalism". But a fundamental tension is inherent in his narrative. In substance, it also knows a "final" side, which Weber characterizes with attributes such as non-formal, material, ethical, political, utilitarian or irrational. However, and without giving too much away, he described the tension between formal and material (final) law differently from Kantorowicz.

Max Weber considered himself a Romanist and understood Roman law as the "foundation" of any "legal education".[7] The fact that his concept of legal rationalization is based on a specific historical narrative has thus far been little recognized in academic circles, and Weber's view of historical contexts should not be confused with Kantorowicz's Epochs of Jurisprudence. Before we return to this point, Weber's idea of rational legal finding must be introduced briefly.

WEBER'S CONCEPT OF LEGAL RATIONALIZATION

"Both law-making and law-finding may be either rational or irrational. They are formally irrational when one applies in law-making or law-finding methods which cannot be controlled by the intellect, for instance when recourse is made to oracles or substitutes thereof. Law-making and law-finding are substantively irrational on the other hand to the extent that decision is influenced by concrete factors of the particular case as evaluated upon an ethical, emotional, or political basis rather than on the basis of general norms. 'Rational' law-making and law-finding may be rational in a formal or a substantive way".

Law is "formal" to the extent that "in both substantive and procedural matters, only unambiguous general characteristics of the facts of the case are taken into account". Law is rational in a substantive way in so far as it

> is influenced by norms different from those obtained through generalization of abstract interpretations of meaning. The norms to which substantive rationality

[7] Max Weber, "Brief an Professor Frensdorff in Göttingen v. 22. Januar 1887", in: Weber, *Jugendbriefe* (1936), p. 215 et seq. This is not contradicted by the fact that Weber, particularly in his early works, frequently referred to Germanic law. Attempts to classify him more as a Germanist from a methodological point of view should be treated with caution; in this vein, see Gerhard Dilcher, *Von der Rechtsgeschichte zur Soziologie. Max Webers Auseinandersetzung mit der Historischen Rechtsschule* (2007), in Dilcher (ed.), *Die Germanisten und die Historische Rechtsschule. Bürgerliche Wissenschaft zwischen Romantik, Realismus und Rationalisierung* (2017), p. 402 et seq. Weber's methodological resistance to the "Germanist party of the Historical School of Law" stands in line with irrationalism and in this respect harmonizes with the critique of the doctrine of Free Law. What appealed to the Germanists as historians as academics was precisely the irrational element stemming from the corporative legal order, i.e., the anti-formal element (WuG, p. 495).

> accords predominance include ethical imperatives, utilitarian and other experiential rules, and political maxims, all of which diverge from the formalism of the external characteristics variety as well as from that which uses logical abstraction. (WuG, 396)

This passage has often been interpreted and just as often misunderstood.[8] It is not only the key to understanding Weber's theory of legal decision but is also the core of his concept of law. Most authors believe they can map Weber's typology on a 2x2 contingency table with two pairs of opposites; rational-irrational and formal-material. Strictly

[8] Of the vast amount of literature, only the following can be mentioned here: Nico Roos, "Antiformale Tendenzen im modernen Recht – eine These Max Webers, diskutiert am Beispiel der Laienfrage", in Stefan Breuer and Hubert Treiber (eds.), *Zur Rechtssoziologie Max Webers* (1984), pp. 233-237; Werner Gephart, *Gesellschaftstheorie und Recht – Das Recht im soziologischen Diskurs der Moderne* (1993), pp. 519-521; Richard Swedberg, *Max Weber and the Idea of Economic Sociology* (1998), p. 91; Hans-Peter Müller, *Max Weber - eine Einführung* (2007), p. 237 et seq.; Hubert Treiber, *Max Webers Rechtssoziologie - eine Einladung zur Lektüre* (2017), pp. 34-40. From the distinctions formulated in the passage cited, a line runs to the question of the validity of law – or, in Weber's words, of the "actual location of 'valid' law." Here, a distinction would first have to be made between governmental law and jurisprudential law. Whereas governmental law sets the rules mandated by an authority standing above society, jurisprudential law has its "location" in the concrete decision of an individual case. A parallel, however, is that jurisprudential law, as Weber understands it, also revolves around "general concepts". His "principles of law" are obtained by "generalization", "logical interpretation of meaning", "abstraction from concreteness", and "syllogistically applicable norms" (WuG, p. 457). This idea of jurisprudential law, formulated in the first half of the nineteenth century by the Historical School of Law, which regularly appears in form of customary law, as Weber rightly pointed out (WuG, p. 508), has been extended by the doctrine of Free Law with the assertion that the "legal principle" is merely "the Secondary" and the decision is the relevant factor. Accordingly, it is inaccurate to speak at all of a finding of law by "applying" general norms to a concrete set of facts, because the products of jurisprudence are "the actual location of 'applicable' law" (WuG, p. 507). Such an approach always draws "conclusions from the particular to the particular" and never strives for "general propositions in order to be able subsequently to deduce from them the norms for new particular cases" (WuG, p. 457). The jurisprudential law of the doctrine of Free Law thus differs from the jurisprudential law formulated by the founders of the Historical School of Law in the first half of the nineteenth century. Such a 'theory of validity', limited to individual cases, cannot be reconciled with Weber's concept of legal rationalization for many reasons. In the following, only a selection of these reasons can be outlined.

speaking, however, the typology comprises six fields. In addition, there is the formal-substantive ["formal-material"] pair, which is not identical with the difference of formal-material ["formell-materiell"]. This is easily overlooked because Weber does not always use the terms "formell-materiell" and "formal-material" consistently: "Formell" refers to procedure, "materiell" to the substantive side of law, in the same way that a distinction is still made today between civil procedure and civil law, criminal procedure and criminal law. A law possesses formal qualities if it is based on "unambiguous general characteristics of the facts of the case". A law possesses material qualities, on the other hand, if it contains "norms of a different qualitative dignity". These include, in particular, "ethical imperatives" or "political maxims" which "diverge from the formalism of the external characteristics variety as well as from that which uses logical abstraction".

Of the six fields, the conceptual pairs "formal-material" and "rational-irrational" are of particular interest here. They promise to shed more light on Weber's understanding of the legal automaton, his narrative of the history of legal science, and his relationship with the doctrine of Free Law and to German studies. In research, the prevailing view is that Weber was a supporter of jurisprudential formalism and the "jurisprudence of concepts". It is true that he did not see unrestrained materialization of the law as an option for modernity and that he appreciated the long dominance of the Historical School of Law as a level of an academic discipline that "had never [been] achieved in any other country".[9] On the other hand, he repeatedly warned against

[9] *Rechtssoziologie* (WuG), p. 495. Weber thus has a different view of matters than, say, Jhering or Kantorowicz. This does not have to mean that the Romanist branch of the Historical School of Law had solved all problems. Weber also did not achieve a "re-systematization of the old law [...] in any convincing way" (ibid., p. 495). Weber's use of the words "begreiflicherweise" or "Neusystematisierung" (but also his criticism of German studies) are to be understood in the light of the positions of his teacher Theodor Mommsen ("Sohn, da hast Du meinen Speer, meinem Arm wird er zu schwer"), which can only be outlined here on the basis of a few key words ("Die Aufgabe der historischen Wissenschaft und die Bedeutung des römischen Rechts", in: id, *Juristische Schriften* (1907), III, pp. 580-600): "that we have a legal system again instead of a bunch of *brocardicis*" (p. 586); "to find the law from the dung that was called law at

the negative side effects of excessive formalism. For this reason, there are authors who believe that his sociology of law should be placed in the vicinity of the doctrine of Free Law.

None of these classifications is correct. Both the formal and the substantive elements are types in absolute terms, each of which constitutes a single concept of law in its own right. Weber's concept of rationalization, on the other hand, was based on the idea that the concept of law contains not only formal or strict elements, but also material, substantive and thus non-strict elements. Indeed, in principle, not only formal but also material law can satisfy the requirements of rationality. Weber's idea of rationalization is thus based on a two-tier concept of law, which, in addition to a strict law (*ius strictum*), can also take into account ethical elements, for instance in the form of equity (*aequitas*). To avoid misunderstandings, it should be added that the non-strict elements are not outside the law, but are part of the law. Strictly speaking, the "ethical imperatives" transform into 'legal ethics' as soon as they are incorporated into law.[10]

In Weber's writings, then, "formalization" acquires a double meaning. On one hand, it appears as an unmistakable sign of legal progress, and on the other, as a risk: formalism can easily turn into irrationalism if it seeks to omit ethics, politics, or utilitarianism as much as possible from the application of law. It is precisely at this point that the metaphor of the automaton for decision-making reveals its true meaning: The subsumption machine represents a monolithic concept of law that ideally separates law and morality in such a way that "valuations", that is, ethical imperatives, *utilitas*, or political maxims, must be excluded from the outset from the finding of law. From this perspective,

the end of the XVIIIth century" (p. 585). "Century law, to find the right, started completely anew" (p. 585); "task for centuries" (p. 581) [own translation]. Weber thus merely warned against placing overly high expectations on the Romanist branch of the Historical School of Law. This remark should not be understood as a critique of the 'jurisprudence of concepts', as is often claimed in the sociological literature (see chapter 4 below).

[10] See Okko Behrends, "Die rechtsethischen Grundlagen des Privatrechts", in: Franz Bydlinski and Theo Mayer-Maly (eds.), *Die ethischen Grundlagen des Privatrechts* (1994), pp. 1-33.

it is clear that the material elements are an indispensable part of Weber's concept of legal rationalization.

RELATIONSHIP BETWEEN THE "FORMAL-RATIONAL" AND THE "MATERIAL-RATIONAL" LAW

What is the relationship between "formal-rational" and "material-rational" law? The starting point for Weber was the thought that "the strictly professional legal logic", the so-called "legal 'construction' can lead to the "expectations of parties [...] often [being] disappointed".[11] He used the definition of "[t]apping of electrical energy" given in §248c of the German Criminal Code and which a layperson "will never understand", as an example to show that the protest by interested parties against professional legal logic will be "ever-recurrent". Weber raised a structural problem when he observed that, without completely renouncing "that formal character which is immanent in it", a jurisprudence can never "be brought into conformity with lay expectation". This "is just as true of the English law which we glorify so much today, as it was of the ancient Roman jurists or has been of the methods of modern continental legal thought". This conflict between formal and material rationality, which has always existed, is to be distinguished from more recent material demands, which are to be understood as the consequence of the "emergence of the modern class problem". They are brought into contact with the law partly by "labor groups" and partly by "legal ideologists" on the basis of "emotionally colored ethical postulates". Strictly speaking, they are norms that are not "juristic" in character, but "are ethical and claim as their legitimation substantive justice rather than formal justice". Weber sees the novelty of these 'materializations' in the fact that they terminate any

[11] *Rechtssoziologie* (WuG, p. 506). In contrast to the doctrine of Free Law, Weber rejected lay justice: "irrational kadi justiz" (WuG, p. 511). That the conflict between popular conceptions of law and expert legal thinking remains in unabated sharpness to this day can be seen in the current discussions about the play and film "Terror" by Ferdinand von Schierach (on this in more detail, see chapter 7, note 7).

relationship with formal law, that is, they put formalism "fundamentally in question".[12]

From this finding, Weber drew a line to the "status ideologies of the lawyers themselves" and named the adherents of the "doctrine of Free Law" who, in principle, identified any kind of formalism with the "legal automaton" and thereby believed that they must allow "not only nonformal but irrational law-finding". In addition, there was the tendency to claim that "case law is superior to the traditional establishment of objective norms". This preference for English law, however, was countered by the claim that "no precedent should be regarded as binding beyond its concrete facts".[13] Weber is correct in

[12] All passages in this paragraph taken from *Rechtssoziologie* (WuG, pp. 506-507).

[13] All passages in this paragraph taken from *Rechtssoziologie* (WuG, pp. 507-508). In §8 of *Rechtssoziologie* [Sociology of Law], Weber discusses the so-called England problem, that is, the question of why England produced rational capitalism even though its law was not characterized by precisely the kind of formalism on which this economic form depends (still worth reading is David M. Trubek, "Max Weber on Law and the Rise of Capitalism", *Wisconsin Law Review*, III (1972), pp. 720-753). Weber's explanations under the keywords: Concentration of the administration of justice in London, extreme costliness of proceedings, denial of justice to the impecunious, economic advocacy interests (WuG, p. 511) cannot be addressed here. At any rate, the chance of predictability in the law was also preserved in England, albeit in different ways, so that modern capitalism could develop "*either*, as in England, where the development of the law was practically in the hands of lawyers who, in the service of their capitalist clients, invented suitable forms for the transaction of business, and from whose midst judges were recruited who were strictly bound to precedent, meaning to *calculable* schemes; *Or* where the judge, as in the bureaucratic state with its rational laws, is an automaton of paragraphs and precedents into whose top the facts and the costs are thrown, so that it can spew out the verdict together with the reasoning at the bottom together with more or less sound arguments — an apparatus whose functioning is by and large *calculable* or predictable". Max Weber, *Parlament und Regierung im neugeordneten Deutschland. Zur politischen Kritik des Beamtentums und Parteiwesens* (1918), in Weber, *Gesammelte Politische Schriften* (1958), p. 323 (emphasis in the original), as well as in WuG, p. 826. As early as 1905, the constitutional lawyer and expert on English constitutional and administrative law Julius Hatschek (1872-1926) picked up on the Heidelberg lecturer and student of Jellinek, Bruno Schmidt, in his use of the metaphor of the subsumption automaton to point out the peculiarities of the continental administration of justice: "In short, on the Continent the judge is, to use Br. Schmidt's apposite comparison, 'a subsumption automaton into which one throws the coins of the concrete facts on the one side in order to then see the verdict fall

that precedents have their own formalism and cannot be a solution for anti-formalists. Many advocates of English law, "often glorified in our country", that is, Germany, were not concerned with the advantages of precedents, but with the complete eradication of formal law. Weber commented drily and disparagingly on the prospects of an independence of material law, using the term "value irrationalism". One consequence of this irrationalism is that the opposing extreme is encouraged, according to which the law is qualified as "mere method" and the judge as a machine, as a "legal automaton".

The "materializations" propagated by the doctrine of Free Law thus have something in common with jurisprudential formalism: Both directions are based on a simple concept of law; whereas formal law erases "life", substantive law erases "form". In contrast, with his concept of law Weber aimed to do justice to both form and life. Thus, he believed that formal law is mostly based on value judgements that originate directly from society, and anyone demanding that judges give a comprehensive account of their real motives for making decisions would be confusing legal criticism with sociological criticism. The "real" motives are often not known to the judges themselves, and even if they can identify them, this does not necessarily mean that they can address them in a professional manner. In any event, the legal method certainly offers judges no assistance in the matter.

On the other hand, in his dissertation on "Handelsgesellschaften" (1889), Weber accused the legal literature of

out on the other side, perfected down to the last detail, by virtue of the legal apparatus working silently within it'". Julius Hatschek, *Englisches Staatsrecht mit Berücksichtigung der für Schottland und Irland geltenden Sonderheiten. Vol. I: Die Verfassung* (1905), I, p. 154. It is unknown whether Weber was familiar with this quote. In any case, the judge as legal automaton can still be found as a putative characteristic of continental European administration of justice in the second half of the twentieth century: "To legal positivism, the judge seemed to be a kind of automaton into which the case was put and which, after some gentle intellectual humming, produces the decision, properly tailored and ready to hand. And the English world largely still sees the judge in continental law in this way today; miraculously, not without a certain degree of envy". Konrad Zweigert, "Zum richterlichen Charisma in einer ethisierten Rechtsordnung", in *Festschrift für Carlo Schmid* (1962), p. 303.

lacking in "economic or even social theory" and criticized its assessments of being merely the "result of abstract construction".[14] In his habilitation thesis on "Römische Agrarangeschichte" (1891), he was also concerned with the relationship between law and reality or, in his words, law in its "practical significance for the development of agrarian conditions".[15] He used the German law of commerce and bills of exchange [Handels- und Wechselrecht] as a model for a successful combination of theory and practice. In these areas, there was a desire to eliminate the formalities of normal legal procedure for the sake of a "settlement that would be both expeditious and better adapted to the concrete case" (WuG, 504). The "self-defeating scientific rationalization of legal thought" must be prevented by practical adaptation of the law. Otherwise, only "a flight into the irrational" remains possible, comparable to an "irrationalization of religion" caused by esoteric currents (WuG, 509). From here, we come full circle to the six-field table: Theory and practice belong together. Weber's concept of legal rationalization contains not only formal but also material elements.

EXCURSUS: WHY MAX WEBER WAS NOT A "CONCEPTUAL JURIST"

An attempt to summarize the core elements of Max Weber's sociology in a few words would center on concepts such as calculability, rationality, formalization, and disenchantment. "The increasing intellectualization and rationalization of modern society" had the consequence that there were

> generally, no mysterious incalculable powers that play into it, that one can rather control all things – in principle – by calculating. This means: the disenchantment of the world. No longer, like the wild ones, for whom such powers existed, one has to resort to magical means in order to control the spirits or to

14 Max Weber, *Die Geschichte der Handelsgesellschaften im Mittelalter. Nach südeuropäischen Quellen* (1889), p. 151. Also in: *Max Weber-Gesamtausgabe, Abteilung I: Schriften und Reden* (2008), I, pp. 109-347 (MWG I/1).

15 Max Weber, *Die römische Agrargeschichte in ihrer Bedeutung für das Staats- und Privatrecht* (1891), p. 1.

> ask them. Rather, technical means and calculation accomplish this.[16]

Disenchantment thus seems to be a consequence of calculability and rationalization, which in turn depend on technical means, formalization, and expert knowledge. Among the fields removed at the earliest stage from everyday understanding and monopolized by "expert knowledge" is the law. Its function is above all to guarantee predictability, in two respects: first, through the predictability of legal decisions and, second, through the enforceability of those decisions by means of the State's monopoly on the use of force. Weber thus combined predictability as a feature of modern law with the need for a reliable force for enforcement: "The tempo of modern business communication requires a promptly and predictably functioning legal system, i.e., one which is guaranteed by the strongest coercive power. [...] The universal predominance of the market consociation requires [...] a legal system the functioning of which is calculable in accordance with rational rules".[17]

Predictability is therefore the hallmark and fate of modern culture. In one of his rare statements on the future development of mankind, Weber was clear that law in particular will meet this fate. "[A]s a result of technical and economic developments", the law's

> character as a specialists' domain [and the expanding notion] that the law is a rational technical apparatus, which is continually transformable in the light of expediential considerations and devoid of all sacredness of content. This fate may be obscured by the tendency of acquiescence in the existing law, which is growing in many ways for several reasons, but it cannot really be stayed.[18]

16 Max Weber, *Wissenschaft als Beruf* (1919), in *Gesammelte Aufsätze zur Wissenschaftslehre* (7th ed.; 1988), p. 594 (emphasis in the original).

17 Max Weber, "Die Wirtschaft und die gesellschaftlichen Ordnungen", in WuG, p. 198.

18 *Rechtssoziologie* (WuG), p. 513.

Weber now ascribed a "rational-systematic character" to this "technical apparatus lacking any sacredness of content". Legal propositions obtained by "analysis" are systematized in such a way that they are a "logically clear, internally consistent, and, *at least in principle,* gapless system of rules, under which, it is implied, all conceivable factual situations must be capable of being logically subsumed lest their order lack an effective guaranty".[19] The word "logical" occurred three times in this formulation in the German original. We recall the legal criticism of Jhering, who doubted that it was possible to foresee "all conceivable facts" in order to be able to subsume them. In this and other similar statements, Weber in fact made frequent use of terminology that usually characterizes a 'conceptual jurist'. Does he conceive of a system concept which is so narrowly defined that the legal practitioner, like an automaton or supposed conceptual jurist, must reach a decision without active intervention? Apart from the concept of material rationality, the argument against this is that the formulation "in principle gapless" also suggests exceptions, ethical imperatives, or political maxims, which the system is open to accept. Weber himself did not comment on whether and to what extent pandectology, such as that practiced by Savigny, Puchta, or the early Jhering, served him as a model for his concept of legal rationalization. Scholars, especially sociologists, have therefore made attempts to subject system designs in Pandectics to closer scrutiny in order to determine whether they achieved a level of formalism that would reveal correspondences with Weber's concept of legal rationalization.[20]

[19] *Rechtssoziologie* (WuG), p. 396 (emphasis added).

[20] See the ambitious but ultimately unconvincing efforts of Roos, note 8 above, pp. 238-246 (early Jhering); Treiber, note 8 above, pp. 150-161 (Puchta). Evaluations of pandectic works presuppose specialized Romanist knowledge, which has become rare today. Otherwise, a degree of formalism could easily be discovered in them, as has already been established. At the least, the special Romanist literature, admittedly difficult to access, would also have to be taken into account. In the light of increasing attempts at interpretation by non-Romanists, a renowned Romanist recently commented: "those who are unable to read music should refrain from judging a score".

Those sociologists concerned with interpreting the matter tend to focus primarily on the strict-legal elements of pandectology, which is not surprising given the discussions of Weber's dependence on the jurisprudence of concepts. However, the moving parts must also be considered, which grant considerable leeway to ethical imperatives, utilitarian rules of expediency, or political maxims. The bipartite nature of the concept of law is the key to understanding the connections between Max Weber's concept of legal rationalization and Pandectics, and this will be the subject of chapter six. In other respects, it can indeed be assumed that Weber was close to the teachings of the Romanist branch of the Historical School of Law. From his objections to the doctrine of Free Law or to German studies, it cannot be concluded that he wanted to postulate the 'conceptual jurist' or the subsumption automaton. Savigny and Puchta, as will be explained, also exercised sharp criticism of a machine-like application of law, and it may be assumed that the Romanist Weber knew the moving parts of their system designs. The parallel with Pandectics is not the degree of formalism, but in the fact that the latter, following the example of classical Roman jurisprudence, attempted to meet the demands of both formal and material rationality. Law, then, possesses only a relative autonomy; it has not only an open beginning, but also an open end.

SUMMARY

Weber's concept of legal rationalization is based on a dual concept of law that includes both a formal and a non-formal element. The two elements have always been in a conflict which is structural in nature and therefore can never be completely resolved. Weber rejected autonomy or isolation for either of the elements. The metaphor of the legal automaton represented the one-sidedness of unrestrained formalization, whereas a merely substantive legal order leads to a kind of irrationalism that would be afflicted with the stains of political arbitrariness and kadi justice. Unlike in Kantorowicz, the final or material elements in Weber's work may come to be discredited: where any connection with formalism is severed, the door opens to irrationalism.

At this point, Weber parted ways with the Germanists. What attracted them "in that field were indeed those irrational and anti-formalistic elements" (WuG, 495). Weber used the label "formal" in quite different contexts, mostly in a positive sense, so that his narrative of formalism certainly does not present a history of decay. On the other hand, it would be simplistic to see Weber only as an optimist of progress. It is true that he sees legal formalism as an unmistakable characteristic of modernity. But he never tires of warning against the negative side effects of excessive rationalism and especially against the specter of irrationalism. It is hardly necessary to add that Nazi jurists were happy to pick up on the groundwork laid by the 'irrational' currents of the doctrine of Free Law or German studies and exceeded Weber's worst fears by far.[21]

[21] In 1914, neither Hermann Kantorowicz nor Max Weber could have foreseen the erosion of the legal order brought about by National Socialism. From the present perspective, however, there can be no doubt that the doctrine of Free Law, striving for a radical eradication of formal law, played into the hands of the National Socialist jurists. The experiences of the twentieth century, with the chaotic consequences of arbitrary rule by the state, have created the preconditions for the forward-looking significance of Weber's concept of law to be properly recognized. Admittedly, he did not openly state anywhere that a "bulwark of civil liberties" could be built with the help of formal law, but the idea is present everywhere in his concept of legal rationalization. This is evident not only in his reservations regarding irrationalism and kadi justice, but also in his recourse to Jhering's famous dictum about form as the "twin sister of freedom": In order to avoid kadi justice, legal science had to "logically process the legal norms once they existed according to *their* formal method" and thereby "withdraw their application from *arbitrariness*", and indeed "also from that form of arbitrariness which dresses itself in the garb of social-ethical consideration", Max Weber, "Besprechung von Philipp Lotmars 'Der Arbeitsvertrag, Bd. I'", *Archiv für Soziale Gesetzgebung und Statistik*, XVII (1902), p. 725 (emphasis in the original).

Chapter 4
Franz Kafka
"It is a peculiar apparatus"

In Germany, 1914 was the year of general mobilization and the year of pessimism when conflict with industrialized machines replaced romantic enthusiasm for war. It was also the year in which Hermann Kantorowicz completed his "Epochs of Jurisprudence" and Max Weber his "Sociology of Law". In October, two months after the outbreak of the First World War, a third text was written, which also refers to an apparatus that may be called a "legal machine" from a broad point of view. This story, which was not published until after the end of the war (1919), was by none other than Franz Kafka (1883-1924), a lawyer by training and by then one of the most important writers in the German language.[1]

THE APPARATUS AS A CLOSED LEGAL SYSTEM

The location of the plot is a small valley on a remote island in the tropics: a distinguished explorer from an unnamed European country accepts an invitation from an officer who wishes to demonstrate a strange machine. "It's a peculiar apparatus" – so begins the story describing the machine, which at first glance is used only to enforce death sentences. It is likely that Kafka drew inspiration from a travel account by the criminologist Robert Heindl (1883-1958), who in "Meine Reise nach den Strafkolonien" ("My Journey to the Penal Colonies"), first published a year before the outbreak of war, described how an assistant executioner designed an execution machine in a penal colony.[2] Heindl was an

[1] Franz Kafka, "In der Strafkolonie", in Kafka, *In der Strafkolonie. Ein Landarzt. Ein Hungerkünstler* (2011), pp. 7-39 – cited hereinafter as SK. Page numbers refer to the English version: *In the Penal Colony/In der Strafkolonie: Bilingual Edition: English - German/Zweisprachige Ausgabe: Englisch – Deutsch* (2017), opened with Adobe Digital Editions.

[2] Connected with Heindl is one of the most important methods of

acquaintance of the renowned criminologist Hans Gross (1847-1915), who had taught criminal law at the Faculty of Law in Prague beginning in 1902. The assumption is that Kafka became aware of Heindl through Gross, whose lectures he attended.[3] There is a parallel with the narrative in that Heindl was commissioned by the German Reich as an explorer to visit penal colonies of the still young colonial power in the South Seas.

Kafka's legal machine was not identical to Heindl's execution machine. In addition to the carrying out the death penalty, Kafka's machine also writes and delivers the judgment. Strictly speaking, judgment, delivery, and execution comprise a unit in the form of a closed legal system invented by the former, now deceased, Commandant of the colony. The Officer explains the individual parts of the legal machine, for which popular terms have since evolved, to the Traveler: "The one underneath is called the bed, the upper one is called the inscriber, and here in the middle, this moving part is called the harrow" (SK, 2). "Now, to enable someone to check on how the sentence is being carried out,

criminal investigation, "dactyloscopy". The relevant passage of "Meine Reise nach den Strafkolonien" published by Ullstein in 1913 reads: "He is just an oddball, a project maker, I would like to say a homebody. He has invented a machine that can behead five people in three minutes without the executioner being required to touch a safety catch. They cut off their own heads by operating the rocking board, which automatically drops the guillotine. Where several patients come one after the other, the second guillotines the first; he has only to put his foot on the plank and the apparatus begins to work" (p. 53, citation begins with "Er ist nur ein Sonderling [...]" in German). Unlike the machine described in Kafka's story, the function of this apparatus is thus limited to the execution itself. One commonality with the narrative is that Heindl also rejects the existing system of punishment, admittedly more for economic reasons and on account of its lack of efficiency, practicability, and profitability. See Walter Müller-Seidel, *Die Deportation des Menschen. Kafkas Erzählung "In der Strafkolonie" im europäischen Kontext* (1986), p. 135.

[3] Hans Gross was the father of psychiatrist Otto Gross (1877-1920), who maintained relations with, among others, the social scientist Else Jaffé, née von Richthofen (1874-1973). Else von Richthofen was the mistress of Max and Alfred Weber, whose companion she became after her husband's death. See Evelyn Höbenreich, *Marianne Webers "Ehefrau und Mutter in der Rechtsentwicklung". Beziehungsmodelle zwischen römischem Recht und deutscher Kodifizierung* (2018); Albrecht Götz von Olenhusen, *Hintergründe zu Max Webers Presse-Enquete und das Presse- und Urheberrecht seiner Zeit* (2015). Specifically on the connections between Gross and Kafka, see Müller-Seidel, note 2 above, pp. 50-71.

the harrow is made of glass" (SK, 7). The bed is entirely covered in a layer of cotton wool, on which the condemned is laid out on his stomach – "naked – of course". The most important element of the apparatus is the fully automatic inscriber. It works based on templates and it controls the harrow, whose sharp needles penetrate the body of the Condemned. Making the harrow out of glass "gave rise to certain technical difficulties". It did, however, succeed after "several attempts": "We didn't spare any efforts" to guarantee the transparency of the proceedings. And now everyone could see through the glass, how the harrow carries out the judgment by writing the text of the law on the back of the Condemned.[4]

[4] Kafka's machine working under glass is reminiscent of Jhering's description of the analytical method of ancient Roman jurisprudence, which he characterizes with the words: "As under transparent glass does the interior of a machine work under our eyes, just as if the mechanism had been built especially for the purpose of instruction, for school lessons; what happens elsewhere merely by way of inner thinking, happens here in the form of a visible external device - in the proceedings of old, one sees the legal relationship, so to speak, going under the knife by which it is to be dissected". Rudolf von Jhering, *Geist des römischen Rechts auf den verschiedenen Stufen seiner Entwicklung, Dritter Theil, Erste Abtheilung* (4th ed.; 1888, p. 14. This passage has been repeatedly referred to in literature on Kafka's work. See Lida Kirchberger, *Franz Kafka's Use of Law in Fiction. A New Interpretation of In der Strafkolonie, Der Prozess, and Das Schloss* (1986), pp. 30-39; Thomas Weitin, "Revolution und Routine. Die Verfahrensdarstellung in Kafkas Strafkolonie", in Arne Höcker and Oliver Simons (eds.), *Kafkas Institutionen* (2007), p. 264. Under the aspects of "transparency" and "form", there may be beginnings of a parallel here. It is only a matter of how far these bear out. Jhering praised this kind of mechanism, emphasized its forward-looking functions, and distinguishd it from a "formal-dialectical separation mania" as it "tends to appear in times of academic impotence as a distorted image of truthful thought". Jhering, op. cit., p. 13. It is precisely this "distorted image of truthful thought" that will later be characterized (and partly by Jhering himself) in terms such as "judgment machine" or "subsumption automaton". See chapter 2 at note 8 as well as chapters 3 and 4). Whether there is a direct model that Kafka's machine is based on has been the subject of much speculation in the literature. See the overview in Csilla Mihály, "Franz Kafka: In der Strafkolonie", in Zoltán Szendi (ed.), *Wechselwirkungen I* (2012), pp. 373-375. Efforts to achieve "transparency" are rather intended to satisfy the (baser) need to assure oneself of one's own (physical and psychological) integrity by witnessing the suffering of others. The procedure obviously intends to ensure that the audience of a spectacle – or rather, as we would say today: bystanders and gawkers – get their money's worth (or are deterred from inappropriate behavior by cruelty).

JUDGMENT OF THE SERVANT: IDENTITY OF LAW AND VERDICT

The execution of the judgment thus begins with the imperative which has been transgressed being "inscribed on the body" (SK, 5). "As it quivers", the harrow "sticks the tips of its needles into the body" of the Condemned (SK, 7). Once it has finished its cruel work, the body is buried in a pit. The Officer describes the machine's technical achievements with great enthusiasm. The operation of its gears could even be described as 'beautiful' if it were not for that infernal shrieking caused by a ground-off gear wheel in the inscriber. The Traveler's interest in such details is limited. He mainly wants to know about the judgment and by which method it was arrived at: "What is the sentence?" The Officer first describes the facts of the case:

> This morning a captain laid a charge that this man, who is assigned to him as a servant and who sleeps before his door, had been sleeping on duty. For his task is to stand up every time the clock strikes the hour and salute in front of the captain's door. That's certainly not a difficult duty—and it's necessary, since he is supposed to remain fresh both for guarding and for service. Yesterday night the captain wanted to check whether his servant was fulfilling his duty. He opened the door on the stroke of two and found him curled up asleep. He got his horsewhip and hit him across the face. Now, instead of standing up and begging for forgiveness, the man grabbed his master by the legs, shook him, and cried out, 'Throw away that whip or I'll eat you up.' Those are the facts. (SK, 6)

So the captain goes to the Officer to press charges. The text states in this regard: "I wrote up his statement and right after that the sentence" (SK, 6). Usually, the accused and the judge struggle to find out the truth about the facts of the case, the measure of guilt and the correctness of the decision. In the penal colony, on the other hand, guilt is established from the start, it is "always beyond a doubt" (SK, 5). Here no discourse, no communication takes place – no arguments are exchanged between the defendant and the judge. As to why the Officer, despite his youth, is allowed to hold the office of judge at all, he explains as follows: "For I stood at the side of our Old Commandant in all matters of punishment, and I also know the most about the apparatus" (SK, 5).

Thus, the claims about the facts of the case are not verified. The judgment therefore lacks the contemplation and establishment of all the actual facts of the case, which is indispensable for a legal conclusion. The reason may lie in the circularity of the proceedings, which reduces the reality of the events to a single point.[5] Establishing the facts of the case is dispensable here because the wording of the sentence consists only of the law, the text of which "is inscribed on his body with the harrow" (SK, 5). Thus, the legal machine only seems to perform its tasks in several steps. In truth, the entire procedure is based on a self-contained, uniform operation: Facts, norm, and judgment are arrived at simultaneously. The criminal charge, transcription and enforcement of the sentence all coincide. "Our sentence does not sound severe," is the opinion of the Officer. For it merely contains "the law" which the convicted person "violated". In the present case, it reads: "Honour your superiors" (SK, 5).

The identity of the law and the judgment marks the pinnacle of any jurisprudential formalism. At this point, Jhering's "judgment machine", Kantorowicz's "thinking machine", and Max Weber's "paragraph machine" meet Kafka's "peculiar apparatus". All these devices maintain

[5] From this side, too, a connection with the legal-historical and early legal-sociological discourses on the subsumption automaton becomes apparent. For, as a rule, only the application of the law to the fixed facts of the case is addressed here. The ascertainment of the facts is not included, in order to be able to claim that the machinery presents a closed system. Thus, formalism has reached a stage where everyday experiences, reality, "life" can no longer be considered. This is the point of approach used today by authors who believe they must specifically emphasize that in the field of legal tech, with the information provided by the party involved, "all circumstances significant to the individual case must be taken into account". See for example Ariane Berger, "Der automatisierte Verwaltungsakt", *Neue Zeitschrift für Verwaltungsrecht*, (2018), p. 1263. Formalism is further evident in the high value that the narrative places on the writing. Writing fulfills quite different functions in jurisprudence that are more or less related to form. These include the role of promulgation as a means of lending a veneer of legitimacy to regulations, decisions, commands, or orders whose content conflicts with the standards of justice. See Stephan Meder, *Ius non scriptum* (2d ed.; 2009).

a maximum distance from "life", from the facts of the individual case, and thus from practice, because in an ideal view of the world they limit the "judge" to merely repeating what is written in law. The problems of this "method" continue to be debated in jurisprudence. At present, the view which seems to prevail is that it is a relic of nineteenth century and subsumption positivist jurisprudence. This type of jurisprudence, as already discussed, is often referred to as "Begriffsjurisprudenz", despite recent research having shown that there was no such thing as "jurisprudence of concepts" in the nineteenth century. Its characteristic is said to be that the user of the law makes the decision "without active intervention".[6]

"Without active intervention" means two things in particular: With no interpretation and no regard for the circumstances of the individual case or – in Max Weber's terminology – with no regard for "material" aspects that might legitimize a deviation from strict law by way of exception. The controversially discussed question of whether a blanket condemnation of the jurisprudence of the previous century is warranted will have to be revisited. In any case, there is no evidence that Kafka harbored reservations about the jurisprudence established in the nineteenth century. Common ground with these jurisprudential discussions, however, can be seen in Kafka's narrative depiction of the clashes between an older, stricter method and a younger, freer direction.

When Jhering, Kantorowicz, or Weber refer to the legal machine as a metaphor for extreme formalism, it is initially irrelevant whether a human decides like an automaton or whether they use an automaton that then passes judgment for them. In Kafka's short story, the Officer operates like an automaton by simply writing the rule "honor your superiors" on the judgment, that is, confining himself to passing off the legal text as a decision without himself examining the circumstances of the individual case, and without any interpretation or other input. This, of course, does not

[6] Kyriakos N. Kotsoglou, "Subsumtionsautomat 2.0. Über die (Un-) Möglichkeit einer Algorithmisierung der Rechtserzeugung", *JuristenZeitung*, LXIX (2014), p. 454. We will return to this topic in the next chapter (see notes 2 and 8).

exclude the possibility that he is at the same time acting as part of a larger legal machinery, and this also differentiates jurisprudence from the automatic decision-making machine in a stricter sense.[7] These findings, however, are only the tip of an iceberg. Kafka's story contains a whole series of other elements that suggest extreme formalism in the proceedings.

EXTREME FORMALISM OF THE PROCEEDINGS

The starting point of the formalism cultivated on the island is simple: The "basic principle I use for my decisions is this: Guilt is always beyond a doubt" (SK, 5). The mere transgression of the rule is considered to be sufficient for a conviction. Justifications or factors in the person of the perpetrator, such as being a minor, unavoidability or insanity, which could justify a reduction of the sentence or an acquittal, are to be disregarded. "The deed kills the man" is the famous legal saying that, according to today's understanding, gives expression to the principle of strict liability:[8] in this formal kind of attribution, which does not differentiate between intent and negligence, the Officer now sees the great merit of his "legal theory"; indeed, without it the machine could probably not function at all. "Other courts" are unable to follow such a principle. "They are made up of many heads and, in addition, have even higher courts above them" (SK, 6). Since the mere transgression of

[7] See Jhering, who, under the title "Der positivistische Jurist - ein gedankenloses Rädchen in der Rechtsmaschinerie" ["The Positivist Jurist - A Thoughtless Cog in the Legal Machinery"], commented in his inaugural lecture in Vienna in 1868: "However, even worse than this external dependence is another danger that threatens jurisprudence not externally but internally: the danger of internal, intellectual dependence, the danger of giving oneself and one's thinking and feeling to the barren, dead law, of becoming a will-less and uncaring piece of the legal machinery, in short, of escaping from one's own thinking". See Okko Behrends (ed.), *Ist die Jurisprudenz eine Wissenschaft?* (1998), p. 50 et seq., 89. Jhering thus did not taint the "judge" here, but the legal system as such with the flaw of the machine (see chapter 2 at note 8).

[8] See for an overview of the topic, Stephan Meder, *Rechtsgeschichte* (6th ed.; 2017), pp. 43-47, 139 ("the deed kills the man") ["die Tat tötet den Mann"]. On the beginnings of a correction of strict law by *aequitas* (to account for individual cases) in classical Roman jurisprudence, see Stephan Meder, *Der unbekannte Leibniz. Die Entdeckung von Recht und Politik durch Philosophie* (2018), p. 59 et seq.

a rule is sufficient for the conviction, any right to a judicial hearing is superfluous. Formalism is also shown in the fact that the Convicted "has had no opportunity to defend himself" (SK, 5). In particular, he is not allowed to point out the inconsistency of a rule that, on one hand, demands [a duty is] "to stand up every time the clock strikes the hour" and, on the other hand, has the purpose of keeping the person "fresh for service". The extreme formalism of the proceedings is furthermore defended with an argument that, as is typical with regard to machines, aims at efficiency:

> The Captain came to me an hour ago. I wrote up his statement and right after that the sentence. Then I had the man chained up. It was all very simple. If I had first summoned the man and interrogated him, the result would have been confusion. He would have lied, and if I had been successful in refuting his lies, he would have replaced them with new lies, and so forth. But now I have him, and I won't release him again. Now, does that clarify everything? (SK, 6)

This "explanation" is also intended to defend the exclusion of discursive elements. Justifications of this kind are needed because the postulate of a mechanical application of the law is disputed in the penal colony. Kafka creates a caricature of a kind of scholastic dispute, the starting point of which is again the apparatus constructed under the leadership of the old Commandant: Even after his death, "the administration of the colony was so self-contained that even if his successor had a thousand new plans in mind, he would not be able to alter anything of the old plan, at least not for several years" (SK, 2). The supporters of the new Commandant, however, are not prepared to accept this, so that the older, strictly formal direction encounters resistance from a younger, less formal one. At its core, this is a parody of a controversy about the administration of justice, a kind of "clash of methods", with the advocates of the "new lenient administration" doubting that the formalism of the older concept of justice would lead to just results (SK, 11). While the Officer's faith in the justice of his trial is now unshakeable, the opponents seem to be gaining more and more ground. Thus, ensues the farce of a political argument, which the Officer characterizes as follows: in the past, the doctrine of mechanical application of the law had reigned unchallenged. Even to this day, he says, it has many adherents, "but no one admits to it". "If you go into a tea house today—that is to say, on a day of execution—and keep your ears open, perhaps you'll hear nothing but ambiguous remarks." These would be "all supporters". Today there are no more "overt supporters" of the procedure. "I am its only defender, just as I am the single advocate for the legacy of the Old Commandant". "Should such a life's work", he pointed to the machine, "come to nothing because of this Commandant and the women influencing him? Should people let that happen?" (SK, 12).

KAFKA'S LEGAL MACHINE AS A NARRATIVE OF HISTORY

One peculiarity of the automaton metaphor is that it is frequently is based on historical images that can vary greatly. Jhering's critique of law, for example, is aimed at a jurisprudence that has sprung from "forms", an allegedly philosophical idealism of the older historical school of law which sought to banish "everyday life" and practice from law as far as possible. Kantorowicz's history of decay, on the other hand, begins much earlier, in the Byzantine era. His thinking machine serves as an antithesis to the supposedly unrestricted finding of law in classical Roman jurisprudence, which declared the facts of the individual case to be the measure of all things. And Max Weber saw formalism as an indispensable feature of all progress, not omitting to warn against the negative side effects of an overstretched rationalism. Kafka, too, cloaked the antagonism between a strictly formal and a less strict, less restrictive direction, which also knows leniency, in the garb of a historical account.

Despite the difference of older and newer proceedings, Kafka's narrative should not be perceived in a chronological sense or even in the sense of a history of progress. In parallel to the discourses of legal history, legal philosophy, and legal sociology, the narrative is rather about different "methods", whereby older ones may well be superior to the more recent ones. This is not changed by the theory, recently resurfaced, that the progress of law consists in its "successive leniency".[9]

This assumption is based on the widespread notion that the cruelties of the European Middle Ages form a counterfoil to the concept of modernity and thus to the epochs of progress. This view overlooks the fact that even Kant, whom many consider to be the decisive thinker of legal modernity, believed that equity was a "mute deity" that "must not be heard".[10] Likewise, Jean Bodin, Thomas Hobbes, and Samuel Pufendorf, to whose State philosophy we shall return, tried to ban "material" elements from law as far as possible. Compared to a rationalist law of reason espoused by such authors, classical Roman law was more "lenient", because, although it revered the rigorous rule of law, it attributed great importance to aspects of equity (*aequitas*). "Leniency" by itself cannot be an option either. Byzantine law, for example, has been criticized for excessive leniency because it encouraged arbitrariness and kadi-justice. Leniency, therefore, is only suitable for use as a seismograph of legal progress to a limited extent, if at all.

In the same vein, Kafka did not tell a story of progress, even though the reader is made aware of many an injustice within formalism. His depiction is confined to a mere description of processes within an event that unfolds in a small, limited circle, aiming only to "demonstrate how it actually was", and thus parodying a manner of historicism or historical positivism that remains influential. This means,

[9] Gertrud Lübbe-Wolff, *Das Dilemma des Rechts. Über Strenge, Milde und Fortschritt im Recht* (2017) (see Meder, note 8 above, pp. 87-89).

[10] For details, see the following chapter under the keywords law of reason, state as machine, mechanistic paradigm, unilinear concept of law limited to the formal element. In the literature on Kafka, the connections with the theme of "state as machine" have been touched upon already. Kafka scholars, however, believe that this topos can be used to make a general statement about the law, a characteristic of which is based on the fact that a judge can generally decide only according to formal aspects. See Hermann-Josef Röllicke, "Wie kommt das Recht ins Gesetz? Kafkas Maschine in der Erzählung 'In der Strafkolonie'", *Coincidentia*, V (2014), p. 370 et seq. In this direction see also Martina G. Lüke, "'In the Penal Colony' and Beyond: Anxieties about Technology in an Era of Increasing Mechanization", *Journal of the Kafka Society of America*, XXXI-XXXII (2007-08), p. 82. Kafka, however, refused to be bound to this interpretation (see also chapter 7, note 7 below).

at least within this narrative, fundamentally refraining from criticism, for legal criticism, as does all analysis, always relies on a point of view that lies outside the event.

TRAVELER'S JUDGMENT OF THE OFFICER AND THE PROCEEDINGS HE PROPAGATES

Just as all the characters in Kafka's narrative, the anonymous Officer and the Traveler are identified only by their social functions or roles. In direct discourse, the Officer seeks to convince the Traveler of the machine's capabilities: "The Traveler was already being won over a little to the apparatus", whereas it remains unclear if this is the perception of the Officer or a comment of the narrator. In a firm belief in the fairness of the proceedings, the Officer comments upon the work of the machine in operation: "Now justice was being carried out." (SK, 13) The Traveler's first misgivings arise when it is revealed to him that the Convicted does not even know his sentence, that he is not allowed to defend himself, nor is the Captain's information verified. "The information about the judicial procedures had not satisfied him" (SK, 6). And further on it is stated succinctly, but again from the perspective of the Traveler: "The injustice of the process and the inhumanity of the execution were beyond doubt" (SK, 11). Nevertheless, the Traveler seeks to maintain his dispassionate stance, limiting himself to contemplative understanding. He disapproves of the inhumanity of the entire proceedings, but as a citizen of a foreign country he does not believe that he is entitled to judge it (SK, 10). "However, he had to tell himself that here it was a matter of a penal colony, that in this place special regulations were necessary, and that one had to give precedence to military measures right down to the last detail" (SK, 6). Whether Kafka, aside from his knowledge of colonial law, was aware of the special law of the 1907 Hague Convention with respect to the Laws and Customs of War on Land, we do not know. According to the martial law in force at the time of World War I, at any rate, war-related atrocities were to be mitigated only to the extent that "military interests permit".[11]

[11] Alan Kramer, "Kriegsrecht und Kriegsverbrechen", in Gerhard Hirschfeld, Gerd Krumreich and Irina Renz (eds.), *Enzyklopädie Erster Weltkrieg* (3d ed.; 2009), pp. 281-292; Oswald Überegger, "'Verbrannte

On the other hand, everything "seemed to indicate that people were asking for his judgment", that is, the Traveler's judgment, "of this trial" (SK, 11). The narrative gradually begins to shift the emphasis from the judgment of the conduct of the Servant to a second judgment – the judgment of the Officer and the proceedings propagated. "But my guess is that with you", the new Commandant "is exposing me to the judgment of a respected foreigner" (SK, 14). Here the Officer seeks to avail himself of all the rights previously denied to the Servant: careful examination and assessment of the facts, the opportunity to defend himself, the impartiality of the "judge", and to know the judgment even before it is announced and enforced by the machine. In addition, there are the persistent attempts to influence the Traveler's decision, even to manipulate him, such as begging him to "to keep as quiet as possible [...] about your verdict on this procedure" (SK, 16). Even before that, the Officer had asked the Traveler to express a positive opinion about the machine to the new Commander. The Traveler refused to do so, but assured the Officer that he would also not speak negatively about the machine in public. Only in private would he express his concerns to the new Commander.

THE JUDGMENT OF THE LEGAL MACHINE AND ITS EXECUTION

When the Officer realizes that the visitor has long since reached his verdict and thus can no longer influence him, he has the baffled Servant released from the machine and re-dress in his previously discarded clothes. The Officer now undresses himself in the Servant's place and climbs naked onto the device, having set the wheels in such a way that the harrow can stab the words "be just" into his back. Once again, therefore, the judgment in the form of the rule transgressed is to be "written on the body" (SK, 5). And again the judgment merely repeats what the rule states. But

Erde' und 'baumelnde Gehenkte'. Zur europäischen Dimension militärischer Normübertretungen im Ersten Weltkrieg", in Sönke Neitzel and Daniel Hohrath (eds.), *Kriegsgreuel. Die Entgrenzung der Gewalt in kriegerischen Konflikten vom Mittelalter bis ins 20. Jahrhundert* (2008), pp. 241-278.

now the machine follows a completely different "logic". This requires some explanation.

Many authors contemporary to Kafka contemplated the relationship between man and machine.[12] The prevailing view was that the machine was supposed to be the extended arm of man, to be a tool, and man was supposed to rule. Aside from the fact that many critical voices warned against domination of machines over humans, contemporary philosophy of the machine was based on a logic of extension, according to which the external originated from an interior and the machine was something external that man had brought forth from his interior, from his spirit. Max Weber, as indicated, wanted to call the machine a "coagulated spirit".[13] Kafka's legal machine is initially also such a rather

[12] See, for example, Max Eyth, "Poesie und Technik. Vortrag gehalten vor der Hauptversammlung des Vereins Deutscher Ingenieure zu Frankfurt am Main am 6. Juni 1904", in Eyth, *Lebendige Kräfte. Sieben Vorträge aus dem Gebiet der Technik* (1919), pp. 1-22; Friedrich Dessauer, *Technische Kultur? Sechs Essays* (1908); Walther Rathenau, *Zur Kritik der Zeit* (1912); Rathenau, *Zur Mechanik des Geistes* (1913). Further references in Stefan Breuer, *Anatomie der Konservativen Revolution* (1993), (2d ed.; 1995), pp. 70-78; Thomas Weitin, *Notwendige Gewalt. Die Moderne Ernst Jüngers und Heiner Müllers* (2003), pp. 43-81; Benno Wagner, "Connecting Cultures. Heinrich Rauchberg, Franz Kafka, and the Hollerith Machine", *Austriaca: Cahiers universitaires d'information sur l'Autriche,* LX (2005), pp. 53-68; Wolf Kittler, "In dubio pro reo. Kafkas 'Strafkolonie'", in Höcker and Simons (eds.), note 4 above, pp. 56-68; Andrea Polaschegg, "Maschinen (nicht) verstehen. Das kollabierte Paradox in Franz Kafkas Erzählung In der Strafkolonie", *Deutsche Vierteljahrsschrift für Literaturwissenschaft und Geistesgeschichte,* LXXXII (2008), pp. 664-670. The research of the French philosopher and writer Raymond Roussel (1877-1933) should also be mentioned in this context. See the references in Michel Foucault, *Raymond Roussel* (1989), pp. 87-113; Hans Ulrich Beck and Harald Szeemann (eds.), *Die Junggesellenmaschine* (2d ed.; 1999), pp. 212-217; Andreas Wolffsteiner, "'... a new human being, half robot and half four dimensional'. Duchamp, Roussel, Maschine", in Helmar Schramm, Ludger Schwarte, and Jan Lazardzig (eds.), *Spuren der Avantgarde: Theatrum machinarum* (2008), pp. 391-406 (for references to Roussel's decision theory, thanks are due to Roberto Ohrt, Hamburg). On mechanization from the point of view of Kafka's work as an administrative lawyer at the Workers' Accident Insurance Institute, which included opinions on the safety of modern industrial machinery, see Klaus Wagenbach (ed.), *In der Strafkolonie. Eine Geschichte aus dem Jahre 1914* (1998), pp. 83-93.

[13] "Coagulated spirit" was also "that living machine which a bureaucratic organization [...] represents". See Max Weber, "Soziologie der Herrschaft", in Weber, *Wirtschaft und Gesellschaft. Grundriß der verstehenden Soziologie,* ed. Johannes Winckelmann (5th ed.; 1985),

ordinary machine. In the proceedings against the Servant, for example, it is set in motion like a large tool in a quite conventional way. "Just look at it!" the Officer calls down to the Traveler. "He jumped up the ladder, turned a wheel, and called down: 'Watch out—move to the side!' Everything started moving" (SK, 9). In contrast, in the proceedings against the Officer, the machine sets itself in motion. It also now works quite differently than before. Not shrieking, but completely noiseless and without the slightest whirring, the mechanism starts and gains speed. As it does so, the gears lift out of the gearboxes and the entire machine seems to want to burst apart and fall to pieces. The needles of the harrow also write differently than before and stab deeper and deeper into the Officer's body, dripping with blood: "This was not the torture the Officer wished to attain. It was murder, pure and simple" (SK, 23).

The narrator's point is that the machine no longer functions according to the logic of extension to fulfill the order of the human as an extended arm, but instead operates on its own decision. The machine is apparently "intelligent" and has not only the ability to distinguish between the two judgments, between the Servant and the Officer, but even makes a third judgment at the end – and passes its own death sentence. Today, we might say that it learns as it transforms input into output. The parallel between, on the one hand, Kafka's legal machine and, on the other, the discourses conducted in the digital age is that it is not always possible to predict with any certainty which output a given input will lead to. In the case of machines capable of still learning after completing their learning phase, it takes considerable effort – insofar as it is possible at all – to predict how a decision will turn out. Kafka's legal machine

p. 835. From here, there are multiple points of contact with the work of his brother, the national economist, sociologist, and jurist Alfred Weber (1868-1958), under whom Kafka earned his doctorate in law in 1906. Alfred Weber discussed the modern bureaucratization of social life in terms of a "giant 'apparatus'", the "rule of the machine", and an increasing mechanization of social processes that seek to "direct mental efforts from inner to outer existence". Alfred Weber, "Der Beamte", *Die neue Rundschau*, XXI (1910), pp. 1321, 1323, 1330. On the connections between Alfred Weber's critique of bureaucracy and Kafka in particular, see Wagenbach, note 12 above, pp. 80, 100-102; Müller-Seidel, note 2 above, pp. 71-80.

is reminiscent of modern information technology systems, which are called "autonomous" because they have the ability to make non-predictable decisions based on artificial intelligence. Unlike conventional mechanical systems, they are no longer mere tools, instead acting in place of humans "in ways that are inaccessible or opaque to human reason and understanding".[14]

Kafka's legal machine, then, must not be confused with a mere tool. A "murder" is very different from an instrument of torture due to the complex moments of will. Moreover, the self-destruction of the machine can only be the result of its own decision. As much as the final scenes of the narration conjure up the specter of machines' domination over humankind, the signs pointing in the opposite direction and suggesting a reconciliation with human reason are abundantly clear. Is the machine not only doing what might be "just" from a point of view outside the narrative? Several arguments are in favor of this: it exacts the "death penalty" on itself, not only because it has exceeded the limits of its functions, but because, with the Officer's death, the proceedings set up by the old Commandant have become obsolete. Even the "murder" itself, however, meets acceptance among the actors: When the Officer begins to undress and stands naked before the Traveler to get on the device, the narrator states: "In his place, the Traveler would not have acted any differently" (SK, 21). Even the Officer himself seems to acquiesce to his fate. After the execution, his face looks at the Traveler "calm and convinced" with open eyes (SK, 23). And the previously condemned servant also understood: "What had happened to him was now taking place with the Officer." This was the judgment of the machine: "A wide, silent laugh now appeared on his face and did not go away" (SK, 21).

[14] John Danaher, "The Threat of Algocracy: Reality, Resistance and Accomodation", *Philosophy & Technology*, XXIX (2016), p. 249 (see also chapter 8 at note 7).

Chapter 5
Retrospective: Critique of the Legal Machine in Friedrich Carl von Savigny

Who "invented" the metaphor of the automaton? Who first used it? Where are its beginnings? Legal scholars tend to provide different answers to these questions. The prevailing view seems to be that the doctrine of Free Law, in opposition to Pandectics, began to conceive of the thinking machine as a terrifying concept and a tale with a history of decay.[15] It is certainly true that, in the wake of Jhering's critique of "conceptual jurisprudence", the subsumption automaton has often been used as a pejorative term for a way of applying the law that is assumed to have prevailed in the nineteenth century.

Jurists of the day were assumed to believe that the application of law no longer required any individual effort,

[15] See, for example, Regina Ogorek, *Richterkönig oder Subsumtionsautomat. Zur Justiztheorie im 19. Jahrhundert* (1986), p. 5 (first establishing the connection between mechanical application of law and jurisprudence of concepts "in the teachings of the *Freirechtsschule*, which contrasted its demand for greater discretion for the judge with the negative image of the subsumption automaton of earlier [positivist] days") [erstmalig hergestellt wurde ...]; Peter Landau, "Die Rechtsquellenlehre in der deutschen Rechtswissenschaft des 19. Jahrhunderts", in: Claes Petersson (ed.), *Juristische Theoriebildung und rechtliche Einheit* (1993), p. 88 (portraying "the 19th-century jurist as a 'subsumption automaton'" is a "turn-of-the-century caricature") [die Darstellung "des Juristen des 19. Jahrhunderts ..."]. In recent academic literature, this view has rightly been disputed, cf. Christoph-Eric Mecke, *Begriff des Rechts und Methode der Rechtswissenschaft bei Rudolf von Jhering* (2018), p. 308 et seq.; Clara Günzl, "Subsumtionsautomaten und -maschinen. Rechtshistorische Anmerkungen zu einem beliebten Vorwurf", *JuristenZeitung*, LXXIV (2019), p. 181 (each with further references). As for the sweeping claims about the nineteenth century, it should suffice to point out that Jhering referred to the machine and automaton metaphor as early as 1868 (see the evidence in chapter 2 above).

that it was sufficient to slavishly adhere to the wording of the law and that a decision could be made without reflection on consequences, that is, without "practice" and without "real life". As "relics of 19th century and subsumption-positivist jurisprudence", jurisprudence of concepts and formalism are labels applied to a 'method' that forces the user of the law to come to a decision "without active intervention".[16] From here, a direct line leads to Kafka's "Penal Colony", where a "repetitive machine" merely restates what is written in the law. Strictly speaking, "without active intervention" means above all two things: Without interpretation and without regard to the facts of the individual case, or, in legal terminology, without regard to good faith (*bona fides*) or equity (*aequitas*), which can justify a deviation from strict law (*ius strictum*) under certain conditions.

CONCERNS ABOUT A MECHANICAL APPLICATION OF LAW IN THE FIRST HALF OF THE NINETEENTH CENTURY

The term jurisprudence of concepts was coined, as noted, by Rudolf von Jhering in the last third of the nineteenth century. Jhering's critique of the law centered on the jurisprudence of the first half of the nineteenth century, and especially the founders and first protagonists of the Historical School of Law, Friedrich Carl von Savigny (1779-1861) and Georg Friedrich Puchta (1798-1848). From today's perspective, the critique is linked to two fundamental and closely intertwined problems. First, recent research has cast doubt on whether a jurisprudence of concepts ever existed. And second, not only Savigny and Puchta but also many other authors of the historical orientation warned against a mechanical application of law and called for a "deautomatisation" of legal decision-making in the first half of the nineteenth century.

[16] Kyriakos N. Kotsoglou, „Subsumtionsautomat 2.0 Über die (Un-)Möglichkeit einer Algorithmisierung der Rechtserzeugung", *JuristenZeitung*, LXIX (2014), p. 454 (see chapter 5). References for literature that still asserts that jurisprudence of concepts dominated the nineteenth century in Stephan Meder, "Rudolf von Jhering und der Aufstand gegen den rechtswissenschaftlichen Formalismus", *JuristenZeitung*, LXXIV (2019), pp. 689-696 (for possible reasons for this dubious claim see note 8 below).

Savigny's resistance to conceiving of legal discovery as a "mechanical process" runs like a common thread through his entire work. Even in early notes not originally intended for publication, he sketched the outlines of his critique: "The judges – too much like machines: the whole legal code is geared to this". Savigny complains about the "mechanical set-up of the judicial process" and the resulting "adherence to the letter". Throughout, he warns against a factory-like production of judgments, and against a mechanical or automatic application of rules to the facts of the case. In his "Vorlesungen über Juristische Methodologie" ("Lectures on Legal Methodology"), which are similarly outlines not intended for publication, the misgivings about such judgment without powers of discernment are summarized in a condensed form: "Most common view, the so-called practical - explanation: Aggregate of legal rules, to be learned immediately and applied as it were mechanically".[17]

From here it is but a small step to the "tact" which Savigny introduced into jurisprudence following debates held in the time of Goethe.[18] The point of origin here is the idea that everyday life constantly produces new cases, that

[17] "Einleitung zu den Pandekten 1821/1822-1823/1824", in Aldo Mazzacane (ed.), *Friedrich Carl von Savigny. Vorlesungen über juristische Methodologie 1802-1842* (1993) (2d ed.; 2004), p. 271 ("Impossibility of achieving the goal in *this* way, founded in the *always newly generating* diversity of cases"). See also Savigny, *Vom Beruf unsrer Zeit für Gesetzgebung und Rechtswissenschaft* (1814), p. 5 ("new codes of law were demanded, which, by their completeness, should grant mechanical security to the administration of justice, in that the judge, deprived of all discretion, would be limited to a literal application"); *System des heutigen römischen Rechts* (1840), I, p. 8 ("this living construction of the legal relationship in any given case is the spiritual element of legal practical work, and distinguishes the noble profession from the mere mechanism that so many ignorant people see in it"). For further evidence, see Stephan Meder, *Urteilen. Elemente von Kants reflektierender Urteilskraft in Savignys Lehre von der juristischen Entscheidungs- und Regelfindung* (1999), p. 43 et seq. Merely in passing, it should be noted that in his critical discussion of Savigny's doctrine of legal sources, Georg Friedrich Wilhelm Hegel (1770-1831), agreed with one point: "That there are collisions in the application of the laws, where the judge's mind has its place, is absolutely necessary, because otherwise the very implementation would become something quite machine-like". Hegel, *Grundlinien der Philosophie des Rechts* (1821), §211 at the end.

[18] See the references in Stephan Meder, *Mißverstehen und Verstehen. Savignys Grundlegung der juristischen Hermeneutik* (2004), for example, pp. 86-88.

the legislator's effort to achieve a complete and intact system without gaps is illusory, and that leeway must be left. With terms like tact, feeling, or power of discernment, the accent is shifted from the letter of the law to the individual effort of the "user of the law", to their ability to grasp the consequences of their decision. "Tact" thus precisely juxtaposes the counter-model of that "most ordinary view" which would like to see in law an accumulation of "mechanically applicable rules". Savigny considered this "view" to be the product of a series of misconceptions, in particular a false doctrine of the origin and source of law. This will be discussed later.

In the first half of the nineteenth century, when jurisprudence of concepts and unrestrained formalism were supposedly dominant, many authors in addition to Savigny or Puchta drew caricatures of the judge as a "repetition machine". Gustav Hugo (1764-1844), founder or at least most prominent exponent of the Historical School of Law, stated, for example, in 1844 "that it would do no good to turn the judge into a mere judging machine". Johann Friedrich Kierulff (1806-1894), member of the Frankfurt Parliament, spoke in 1839 of an "old unscientific view that entertains the idea of a mechanical certainty in the field of law as a possibility". And Georg Beseler (1809-1888), an adherent of the Germanic branch of the Historical School, polemicized a little later in all severity against a "rigid system of forms" and the "fabrication of judgments that merely grasp external factors".[19]

[19] Machine application of law as mere repetition of the law: Georg Friedrich Puchta, *Vorlesungen über das heutige römische Recht. Aus dessen Nachlaß*, ed. Adolf August Friedrich Rudorff (1847), I, §§5-9, p. 17 ("it may well be that some legislators have adopted the idea that only they need knowledge and mind; the judge can then be a simple repetitive machine"). Mechanical Application of Law versus Equity [Billigkeit]: Gustav Hugo, *Rezension Schlosser Briefe über die Gesetzgebung überhaupt, und den Entwurf des Preussischen Gesetzbuchs insbesondere* (1789), in *Beyträge zur civilistischen Bücher-Kenntniß der letzten vierzig Jahre* (1828), I, p. 114 ("much was left to this equity in the whole of the fine Roman Law and in this respect, too, the simple historical remark makes it very probable that one would not be well advised to consider the judge a simple judgment machine reduced to looking up the case in the very detailed law books or the Pandects, in order to see it decided *in terminis*"). In this vein, see also Georg Beseler, *Volksrecht und Juristenrecht* (1843), p. 261 ("this consideration of actual circumstances, on which the rule of *bona fides* is based, is indispensable unless one wishes for, instead of

This list could be continued without difficulty. We will, however, follow a different lead that ties in with an already-quoted phrase from Max Weber, in which he said the legal machine appears "subaltern" to modern jurists and is "felt to be increasingly embarrassing precisely because of the universalization of codified formal law".[20] Weber thus assumed that there had once been a time when such machines were not perceived as embarrassing, but were regarded as normal or even desirable. Anyone asking the question at the beginning of the twentieth century as to when the legal machine had gained such acceptance would have heard the same reply from many an academic jurist: at the times of jurisprudence of concepts in the first half of the nineteenth century! It can, however, be easily shown from the sources and from the results of recent research that this answer cannot be correct. Therefore, an opinion had to have existed even prior to that, namely in the eighteenth century, which considered mechanical certainty in the finding of law to be possible and desirable.

Contemporary literature presents ample evidence that such a view actually existed; in other words, that there was an age in which the machine ideal was regarded not as an embarrassment but as normality. Kierulff, for example, spoke of an "old unscientific view" and Savigny of a "most ordinary view" whose adherents believed they could apply legal rules "in a mechanical way, as it were". But who were these supporters? The criticisms were aimed against the rationalistic natural law and the law of reason

a living breathing justice that penetrates the essence of all things, a rigid formality or even a judgment fabrication of a superficial routine that only grasps externalities"). See further: Johann Friedrich Kierulff, *Theorie des Gemeinen Civilrechts* (1839), I, p. XXIX (no leeway according to the "old unscientific view, which considers mechanical certainty in the field of law a possibility, and regards memorizing and copying as a real theory, and application based on craftsmanship as a real practice. Real jurisprudence is legal art, free creation and production"). Further evidence in Mecke, note 1 above; p. 309; Günzl, note 1 above, pp. 185-187. On the image of the judge as an automaton, see also the references in Wolfgang Kilian, *Juristische Entscheidung und elektronische Datenverarbeitung. Methodenorientierte Vorstudie* (1974), pp. 3-5.

[20] Max Weber, *Rechtssoziologie* (1922), in Weber, *Wirtschaft und Gesellschaft. Grundriß der verstehenden Soziologie,* ed. Johannes Winckelmann (5th ed.; 1985), p. 507 (see chapter 4 at note 3).

and against the political imagery of enlightened absolutism, which considered the State a clockwork device, a machine, an apparatus – or as Thomas Hobbes had it in "Leviathan" – an automaton. "Why [is there] any talk of historical school or method at all, since the historical is only one of several necessary requirements?" Savigny answered his own question, "that in the period *immediately preceding* the period in question, historical treatment had been mainly disregarded, so that the reintroduction of this method became the characteristic of the following period".[21] The answer shows that resistance to the mechanistic paradigm of rationalism provided the actual impulse for the establishment of the school and that 'historical' is not sufficient to describe its objectives. That this is where resistance to what was later called the "subsumption automaton" begins, may be briefly explained on the basis of Savigny's legal criticism.

DIFFERENCES BETWEEN THE RATIONAL-LEGAL AND THE "HISTORICAL" ORIENTATION

Even though the doctrine of Free Law began to sound outdated quite quickly, the connection between the legal machine and "jurisprudence of concepts" has stood the test of time. It continued to dominate in the second half of the twentieth century and lives on in weakened state to this day. Only in recent years has the image of nineteenth-century jurisprudence begun to change. More recent works on the history of law and centering on Savigny, Puchta, or Windscheid have challenged the notion that the formalism of the Historical School of Law and Pandectics ever truly existed as academic literature has claimed.[22] Of particular

[21] Savigny, "Einleitung zu den Pandekten 1827/1828-1841/1842", in Mazzacane, note 3 above, p. 286 (emphasis added).

[22] The beginning is a work on Windscheid which claims that his name stands for the "anemic conceptual jurisprudence in the form of rationalist legal positivism" (in contrast, see Ulrich Falk, *Ein Gelehrter wie Windscheid. Erkundungen auf den Feldern der sogenannten Begriffsjurisprudenz* (1989)). In a similar vein, Savigny's theory of hermeneutics has been associated with conceptual jurisprudence by such prominent authors as Hans-Georg Gadamer (against this view, see Meder, note 4 above; see also note 15 below). Three monographs have been published in quick succession on Puchta, always the focus of controversy: Hans-Peter Haferkamp, *Georg Friedrich Puchta und die "Begriffsjurisprudenz"* (2004); Thomas Henkel, *Begriffsjurisprudenz und*

interest here are the conclusions that can be drawn for the automata metaphor from recent academic findings. It has been stated that one of the main features of the jurisprudence of concepts supposedly practiced in the first half of the nineteenth century was that the legal practitioner was required to make a decision "without active intervention".

"Without active intervention" here is a negative way of expressing the application the law in a way that no longer requires any human effort, but rather generates results by way of a mechanical formalism. As a tried and tested means of conducting a litmus test for such formalism, equity (*aequitas*) and interpretation can be considered. This is because the more a decision theory excludes equity and interpretation, the more formal it is. Conversely, and following Max Weber's terminology: The greater the room that equity and interpretation can occupy in the finding of the law, the more "material" it is. In the context of equity and interpretation, therefore, those ingredients come into play that differentiate the subsumption automaton from a verdict that seeks to do justice to the circumstances of the individual case. At the same time, those ingredients divide the rationalistic law of Reason and the Historical School of Law.

That the Historical School can differ considerably from the school of "natural law" has often been mentioned. Therefore, only a few lines of difference will be recalled here which separate the two schools of thought. Among the ideas at the root of many natural law doctrines is the narrative

Billigkeit. Zum Rechtsformalismus der Pandektistik nach G.F. Puchta (2004); Christoph-Eric Mecke, *Begriff und System des Rechts bei Georg Friedrich Puchta* (2009). One can only speculate about why legal research has been resistant to these findings and why the assertion of a connection between the legal machine and conceptual jurisprudence has survived to the present day (see note 2 above). Perhaps one reason is that jurists have difficulties in making consensual statements about the functions of legal thought and method. Thus, it is advisable to use a "method" on which, despite it never existing, there is consensus that it should be rejected. Or to put it differently: Jurisprudence invents a "method" that it does not want because of the difficulty it has in expressing what it does want. The doctrine of the jurisprudence of concepts would then take on the function of being the scapegoat on which legal science and jurisprudence could focus (or project) their desire for consensus on legal thinking and method.

of the natural state and of the social contract, on which such diverse authors as Hobbes, Pufendorf, Thomasius, Rousseau, and Kant base their philosophy of law and the State. As is well known, Hobbes described the natural state as a state of war, which was only ended by the transition into a state of law. "Homo homini lupus" found it necessary to establish a social contract, the purpose of which was to secure peace and protect private ownership through the consensual transfer of undivided power to *one* sovereign.[23] According to this narrative, the State, polity, or legal order do not exist from the outset, but are only artificially created by a consensual expression of will, and this is the social or subjugation contract. The result is the dissolution of every creation of norms which might exist outside of law of the state, for example, through common law or academia. Savigny criticized the attempts to monopolize law in statutes and counters the voluntarism of an etatistic theory of the source of law with his idea of the plurality of sources. He rejected the doctrine of the natural state as mere fiction, as he did not accept that "in the existence of peoples" there was a "time before the invention of the state".[24]

Savigny's critique of law is directed against the State-philosophical positivism that prevailed in the seventeenth and eighteenth centuries, which wanted to consider even extremely unjust laws to be the law and to eliminate those principles of checks and balances that were traditionally gathered under the concept of *aequitas*. Thus, equity sinks below the orders of the sovereign already in Bodin: "A legal prohibition is stronger than even overt demands of equity." Hobbes, Pufendorf, or Kant also targeted equity because

[23] On this and the following, see the references in Stephan Meder, *Doppelte Körper im Recht* (2015), pp. 25-27, 89-91, 86-94, 119-120; 321-328; Barbara Stollberg-Rilinger, *Der Staat als Maschine. Zur politischen Metaphorik des absoluten Fürstenstaats* (1986); Ethel Matala de Mazza, *Der verfasste Körper. Zum Projekt einer organischen Gemeinschaft in der Politischen Romantik* (1999). An exception is Leibniz, whose historical natural law exhibits many points of contact with the teachings of the Historical School of Law. See Stephan Meder, *Der unbekannte Leibniz* (2018), pp. 279-311.

[24] Savigny, *System des heutigen römischen Rechts*, note 3 above, p. 9 (p. 23).

"a judge cannot rule based on indeterminate conditions".[25] They excluded the empirical level when they deny that the specific facts of a particular case can perplex formal law. In doing so, they strain the law of the State and accept that the "highest law leads to the highest violation of law". In the aphorism *"summum ius summa est iniuria"* that experience

[25] Jean Bodin, *Sechs Bücher über den Staat* (1576), ed. Peter Cornelius Mayer-Tasch (1981), I 8 (p. 231); Immanuel Kant, *Metaphysik der Sitten* (1797), in Kant, *Werkausgabe* (10th ed.; 1993), VIII, pp. 341-342 and 326. It is still a widely held view that the modern Law of Reason, and especially Kant, established "modernity" in private law with the person at the center and subjective rights. It is true that thinkers such as John Locke, Thomas Hobbes, Samuel Pufendorf, Gottfried Wilhelm Leibniz, Moses Mendelssohn, and Immanuel Kant all postulated freedom, life and personal ownership as inalienable rights of citizens. With the exception of Leibniz, the majority of authors of the Law of Reason have anchored the demarcation of individual rights of freedom (autonomy, subjective rights) in the concept of the social contract. Savigny, as far as the granting of liberty rights is concerned, is in agreement with the Law of Reason, but rejects the idea (prevailing in the Law of Reason) of a merely formal liberty with the doctrine of the social contract. See Meder, note 9 above, pp. 25-27, 89-91, 321-328. In particular, he rejected the separation of jurisprudence from morality, which is so important for the subsumption automaton and other legal machines (chapter 7), and the banning of equity with its rigorous renunciation of individual case justice, which not least also characterizes Kant's legal philosophy and which – with good reason – has recently been interpreted again as the depersonalization of law, the demise of the subject, or the erosion of the anthropocentric system. See Frederik von Harbou, "Abschied vom Einzelfall? - Perspektiven der Digitalisierung von Verwaltungsverfahren", *JuristenZeitung*, LXXV (2020), p. 348 (see also chapter 7 at note 17 and chapter 9 at the end). Against this background, the traditions oriented towards Roman law appear more "modern" than most rational-law theories for (at least) two reasons. First, because Roman law, with its three-part division of the material into *persona, res,* and *actio,* made a demarcation of spheres of freedom (see Jan Schapp, *Methodenlehre des Zivilrechts* (1998) pp. 53-63), which is able to take sufficient account not only of the "person" (or absolute and relative subjective legal positions), but also of the material elements of law (*aequitas,* proportionality, individual case justice, and others). And second, because this approach has remained vindicated vis-à-vis the one-pillar conceptions formulated in the seventeenth and eighteenth centuries. This is because nowadays few would deny that, in addition to *ius strictum,* legal concepts such as *aequitas, bona fides,* proportionality, or similar can also play a decisive role in jurisprudence. The question remains of how the modern research on Kant could disregard these findings (see only the section on "Billigkeit und Notrecht" in Otfried Höffe, "Der Kategorische Rechtsimperativ. 'Einleitung in die Rechtslehre'", in: id., *Immanuel Kant, Metaphysische Anfangsgründe der Rechtslehre* (1999), pp. 58-62, or Philipp-Alexander Hirsch, *Kants Einleitung in die Rechtslehre von 1784* (2012)) and still tends to emphasize the "Kantian influence" on Savigny (for example, Höffe, op. cit, p. 17).

has become proverbial which Kant must exclude from his formal concept of freedom taken from reason alone.

INTERPLAY OF FORMAL AND MATERIAL ELEMENT IN SAVIGNY'S CONCEPT OF LAW

Thus, while Kant accepted that "*summum ius*" can be "*summa iniuria*", Savigny distinguished between a "pure" legal principle, which creates formal jurisdictions, and a "mixed" legal principle, by virtue of which material aspects can also come into play. Referring to evolved Roman jurisprudence, he claimed that law is impossible without structural formalism, but that formalism requires a corrective instrument called *aequitas*. These "two elements of the law" not infrequently "appear in a particular opposition to each other, fight and limit each other reciprocally, in order to perhaps resolve themselves into a higher unity in the future".[26] Savigny thus considered the conflict between formal and material aspects to be a fundamental condition of all law. Despite this, even after 1968 the opinion still prevailed that "equity as a category of law had been eliminated" in the nineteenth century. It was sufficient to refer to the authority of Kant, whose separation of "law and morality as independent spheres" was generally accepted in the nineteenth century.[27] Under the premises of a formal and conceptual jurisprudence dependent on the ideal of the

[26] Savigny, *System des heutigen römischen Rechts,* note 3 above, §15 (pp. 54-56); §22 (p. 112); §59 (pp. 407-410). In more detail Okko Behrends, *Struktur und Wert* (1990), in Behrends, *Institut und Prinzip* (2004), I, pp. 58-60. Savigny was by no means alone in arguing that with *aequitas,* social and consequently material aspects could also be included in law. Similar (and in some cases more extensive) approaches can also be found in many other authors of the nineteenth century, of whom Baron, Regelsberger, and Dernburg should be highlighted in addition to Puchta. See Stephan Meder, "*Aequitas* und *ius strictum* in der Historischen Rechtsschule und Pandektistik", in Matthias Armgardt and Hubertus Busche (eds.), *Recht und Billigkeit* (2021). Material elements, especially as equity is in the end a collective term, can still enter through many other channels. As examples, Savigny mentioned *aequitas, naturalis ratio,* the nature of things or *ius gentium*: *publica utilitas, ratio utilitatis, bona fide,* good morals (*boni mores*), and other indeterminate legal concepts. Savigny, *System des heutigen römischen Rechts,* note 3 above, pp. 55-66.

[27] Clausdieter Schott, "Aequitas cerebrina", in *Rechtshistorische Studien. Hans Thieme zum 70. Geburtstag zugeeignet von seinen Schülern* (1977), p. 139.

machine, this statement must have seemed plausible. It was to take some time before legal historians began to become suspicious.

The same applies with regard to interpretation: The more restrictively a legal doctrine handles interpretation, the more "mechanical" it is. For instance, the theory of legal sources in the theory of the Law of Reason, which recognizes only formal law, tends to warn against the dangers of interpretation and even recommends it be excluded altogether. Just recall Hobbes's indignation at the arbitrariness of jurists who interpret, or the ban on commentary in the 1794 Prussian Allgemeines Landrecht.[28] Enlightened absolutism and State-philosophical positivism wanted to limit the judge to the letter, to the wording of the law. Savigny's model of legal hermeneutics has also been accused of formalism. His hermeneutics could not meet modern demands, since it degrades the judge to an "executor of the law" and the judgment to a "mechanical copy of the portion of life to be decided on".[29]

This criticism fails to recognize that Savigny's doctrine of the four *canones* deprived the "letter" of its prevalence in the doctrine of interpretation. All four elements have equal rank and serve only as aids to the now "free" determination of the "thought" of the legislator. Moreover, Savigny never tired of emphasizing the productive character of interpretation. For the "thought" must be reconstructed for every law "when it intervenes in life." Elsewhere the allegedly conceptual jurist says "we must add something to it from our side when a regulation is to enter into everyday life".[30] According to Savigny, it is precisely social reality that

[28] See chapter 26 of Hobbes, *Leviathan* (1651). In a similar vein, Jhering's admired founder of classical utilitarianism, Jeremy Bentham: "Wenn sich der Richter untersteht und die Macht anmaßt, die Gesetze zu interpretieren, so wird alles völlig unberechenbare Willkür". Bentham, *Works*, ed. John Bowring (1838), II, p. 325.

[29] See Ernst Forsthoff, "Hermeneutische Studien", in: *Recht und Sprache* (1940), pp. 23-31. Similarly, Hans-Georg Gadamer in *Wahrheit und Methode* (1960), whose arguments against Savigny's hermeneutics depend largely on Forsthoff. For details, see Meder, note 4 above, pp. 1-8.

[30] Savigny, *System des heutigen römischen Rechts,* note 3 above, for

challenges the interpreter to say more than has already been said. Today we would – depending on the situation – refer to productivity, concretization, or material justice. Having recourse to "life" indicates that the hermeneutics are open to empiricism, which results in a considerable expansion of the scope of interpretation, a shift of emphasis away from the legislative will to the interpreter's own individual character and to social reality itself. Therefore, it is unsurprising that Savigny frequently spoke of tact, feeling, art, or judgment. This is precisely where we find Savigny differing from Jhering, who paid no comparable attention to hermeneutics or to the doctrine of interpretation or equity.

COMPARING CONCEPTS OF LAW: SAVIGNY VERSUS KANT, JHERING, KANTOROWICZ, AND WEBER

Savigny formulated a two-tiered concept of law, which can be characterized as a kind of philosophical dualism – as a dichotomy, difference, or even incommensurability of law and equity.

In this context, he never failed to draw attention to the importance of material elements of law for the legal method of further developing the law. The integration of equity has, he argued, led to entirely new legal solutions, from which independent legal institutions have emerged over time and will continue to emerge in the future. In contrast, Kant's legal thinking was based on a single source doctrine, according to which equity is a "mute deity" that "cannot be heard". His use of "hear" indicates that equity does have the potential for producing sound. It produces a buzz, a murmur, and thus irritates those charged with judging cases on the basis of formal law. But according to Kant, the judge must follow the tracks of the rigid rule of law and may not create any new paths: He must pretend not to hear, must ignore all noises, signals, or warning signs to the point that one day,

example §32, pp. 207 and 206. Consequently, his interpretations also contain the legal method of further development of the law by judges in which material elements play a role (*aequitas hermeneutica*), for example, ibid., §37, pp. 235-236. Although Puchta's doctrine of interpretation differed from Savigny's, he too granted the interpreter degrees of freedom that a formalist would never allow.

perhaps, a legislator must consider establishing a new rule. Bodin, Hobbes, or Pufendorf were of a similar opinion. They all propagate a one-tier legal concept that recognizes only the formal side and denies judges any of the leeway which is indispensable if the circumstances of a case are to be taken into account. This kind of approach cannot harmonize ideally only with the image of the State as a machine but also with the postulate of a mechanical application of the law.

The theory of sources in enlightened absolutism was thus based on the premise that the law resides in the legislation of the State, whereas the Historical School of Law began to postulate the model of jurisprudential law. In this model, the law of the State is only one – albeit an important one – among several sources of law. Jurisprudential law resides not in the orders of a sovereign will, but in the concrete decision regarding an individual case. Practical application of the law mostly resorts to jurisprudential law when legal rules are found wanting or when they lead to unjust results. As Max Weber noted, since it requires a specific legitimation, jurisprudential law will regularly appear in the form of customary law.[31] This conclusion gives reason to return to the question posed at the outset: who first criticized the automaton? In the nineteenth century, it was probably Savigny who first spoke in a pejorative sense of the "machine", "judgment factories", or the "mechanical application of law". The expression "subsumption automaton", on the other hand, appeared much later. It is thought to have originated with the Heidelberg scholar and student of Jellinek, Bruno Schmidt (1865-1905), who in his paper on "Das Gewohnheitsrecht als Form des Gemeinwillens" (1899) first astonished the readers of the day with the assertion that customary law would be created only if a user of the law exceeded the limits of their competences. The State can either object to this behavior or tacitly accept it. If it remains silent and the *communis opinio* accepts the decision, new law arises in the form of customary

[31] Weber, *Rechtssoziologie*, note 6 above, p. 508. So, too, the BGB drafters and the followers of the Historical School of Law after the turn of the nineteenth century. See Benno Mugdan (ed.), *Die gesammten Materialien zum Bürgerlichen Gesetzbuch* (1899; reprint 1979), I p. 570.

law. To avoid misunderstanding, Schmidt also added that whoever renders a legal decision must be allowed a certain amount of leeway in general. Schmidt used this statement, which was by no means self-evident after the establishment of the German Empire, at least with regard to public law, as the occasion to make a memorable comment that sheds light on the complex connections between the automaton of subsumption, jurisprudence, and customary law:

> It would be a fatal error to believe that in even the smallest state, the legislation could be so detailed and elaborate that it would contain in advance every decision for every possible occurrence of practical life, and that consequently the subordinate bodies would have to confine themselves merely to the application and execution of the already existing social will. This is not possible even with regard to jurisdiction, even though here most people see the sole solution in the demotion of the judge to a machine-like 'subsumption' automaton, into which one throws the coin and the facts of the case, in order to then see the decision, perfected down to the smallest detail, fall out on the other side by virtue of the law apparatus working silently in it.[32]

[32] Bruno Schmidt, *Das Gewohnheitsrecht als Form des Gemeinwillens* (1899), p. 15 ("this view is practically refuted by the numerous cases in which the law itself expressly refrains from determining the decisions that have to be made in the future down to every detail"). Erich Jung, *Das Problem des natürlichen Rechts* (1912), p. 13; see the referemces in Günzl, note 1 above, p. 182, is of the opinion that Bruno Schmidt first used the term "Subsumtionsautomat" (subsumption automaton). As noted above, Julius Hatschek adopted Schmidt's expressions (chapter 4, at note 13). Although Schmidt, however, considers it impossible that a judge can ever be a subsumption automaton, Hatschek refers to this metaphor in order to point out the difference between German law and English law. In the field of Comparative Law, the relation to conceptual jurisprudence is thus abandoned and the "subsumption automaton" is stripped of its negative connotations (for further examples in the relevant literature in chapter 4, see note 13). In his role as a constitutional lawyer, Hatschek takes this a step further. According to the principle of the Separation of Powers, the "judge must be a 'subsumption automaton'" because otherwise he would usurp legislative powers. See *Englisches Staatsrecht mit Berücksichtigung der für Schottland und Irland geltenden Sonderheiten: Die Verfassung* (1905), I, p. 157 ("this already follows from the theory, which wants to separate jurisdiction from legislation with a sharp distinction. If the judge were to be more than just a mere applicator of the law, he himself becomes the legislator! This must be avoided at all

Just as Savigny, Schmidt thinks that striving for completeness and comprehensiveness is an illusion because not all events can be foreseen and life constantly produces new cases. Judges must therefore be allowed some leeway to exercise their productive power of judgment. To deny this would be to demote the judge to a "machine-like 'subsumption' automaton", and this closes the circle to the logic of the machine model: The epoch of the Law of Reason had to banish equity from the law by asserting that a judge "cannot pronounce according to indeterminate conditions". Their understanding of the law was not able to allow to jurisprudence the leeway which such different authors as Savigny or Schmidt considered indispensable.

One characteristic of jurisprudence is its capacity to abstract and form general concepts. Such a formation of concepts beyond the formal legislation process does have formal character, as long as it is recognized by the *communis opinio*. This type of formal law can also, under certain circumstances, be supplemented or corrected by the judge's own additions. So, here, too, mechanical application of the law is out of the question. Thus: Savigny developed a two-pronged concept of law in which formal and material elements interact. There is a certain connection between the classical doctrine of jurisprudential law and the doctrine of Free Law insofar as the latter assumes that law resides primarily in the concrete decision of an individual case. However, the doctrine of Free Law – revealing the fundamental difference – "always proceeds from the specific to the specific" and never strives for a conclusion of "general propositions" in order to establish a solution on the basis of these propositions.[33] Like the law in England, then, the doctrine of Free Law does not want to claim application of general norms to the specific facts of the case. Rather, it is the other side of the secular law of reason, as it seeks to eliminate any formal elements. Admittedly, the doctrine of Free Law also advocates a singular concept of law. It is just

costs"; Schmidt also speaks of transgressing the boundaries, only that he draws different conclusions.) Even today, there are still quite a few authors who assess lawmaking beyond the state on the basis of a "*legal centralism*", see Meder, note 9 above, for example, p. 250.

33 Weber, *Rechtssoziologie*, note 6 above, p. 457.

that this singular concept consists not of the formal but of the material element of law.

Given Jhering's wavering between condemning and praising formalism, he would probably have rejected the legal terminology of the doctrine of Free Law. He by no means understood form solely in a pejorative sense. Here it is only necessary to recall his famous phrase: "Form is the sworn enemy of arbitrariness, the twin sister of freedom". On the other hand, he sharply criticized the "jurisprudence of concepts" with its assumed formalism. Also, the idea of "purpose" he propagated can be easily hijacked by arbitrariness – for non-formal and irrational formations of law.[34] Scholars have long and often puzzled over how to explain this "dichotomy". It is sufficient to note here that, in view of his continual wavering between extreme positions, it is not possible to say unequivocally whether Jhering would have preferred a singular or binary concept of law.

Max Weber, on the other hand, showed a straight edge with his concept of legal rationalization. He saw formalism as an indispensable feature of modernity, without failing to warn against negative side effects: the excessive formalism of a "legal machine" can quickly slide into the irrational. Since not only formal but also material elements are capable of fulfilling the requirements of rationality, Weber constructed his sociology of law on the basis of a binary concept of law that is capable of taking into account not only strict law but also political maxims or ethical imperatives, for instance in the form of equity. As a result, we can note: Savigny and Weber agree on one central point; both developed binary concepts of the law. One difference, however, is that Savigny, as will be explained in the following chapter, looked more closely at the question of the relations between formal and material elements of law.

[34] See the references to the appropriation of Jhering's "purpose" by Nazi jurisprudence in Meder, note 2 above, p. 691.

Chapter 6 Algorithms between Calculability and Valuation: "Revisiting" the Relationship between Law and Ethics

Can technology replace clear judgment? Are the days in which humans sit in judgment over other humans numbered? When will the vision that lawyers are no longer needed become a reality? These questions have been asked for some years in an almost unmanageable flood of publications on "legal tech".[1] And indeed, there are a multitude of areas in which it seems possible that legal decisions can be reached based on a few parameters without regard to the individual person. Some examples are cited over and over again: penalizing road traffic violations or automatic assessment of claims for damages such as reimbursement claims for delayed flights on the basis of the European Union Passenger Rights Regulation. On the other hand, judges must fill in incomplete facts and indeterminate legal concepts, exercise their discretionary power, make evaluations, and sometimes decide *praeter* or even *contra legem* in order to meet the requirements of "justice". The requirement for a judgment tends today to be seen as the strongest argument in favor of legal decisions remaining the preserve of human competence in the future.

Evaluations and assessments often play a role in everyday legal life, where the task is to separate the relevant data from the irrelevant in order to determine the facts of the case. The

[1] See only the title of the "global bestseller" by Richard Susskind, *The End of Lawyers? Rethinking the Nature of Legal Services* (rev. ed.; 2010). For further evidence, see the next chapter.

"rules" that could support a decision need to be considered simultaneously with the "facts" of the case. In practical application, therefore, we are dealing with a procedure in which the judicial gaze is continually traveling back and forth between the facts of life and the norms that are potentially applicable.[2] But even if a suitable norm has been found, the decision is far from finished. It must be subjected to another examination, this time taking a holistic view that is warranted for many reasons: in the name of public acceptance, in order to identify unjust hardships of formal law, to further the development of the law by judges and, in extreme cases, to allow a *contra-legem* decision leading to a change of law.

How quickly the judiciary can find itself in such an extreme situation will be demonstrated presently by means of a simple example from current legal practice. First, it is sufficient to note that the requirement for evaluation is seen as the main problem when it comes to the question of whether algorithms will be able to take the place of human decisions in the future. The concept of evaluation is to be understood in a broad sense of situational openness. It corresponds in essence to the ethical imperatives, utilitarian rules of expediency, or political maxims that Max Weber used to distinguish material rationality from formal rationality.

FORMAL RATIONALITY OF THE MACHINE

The distinction between formal and material elements of law is the main theme that will guide the following discussion: what conclusions are to be drawn from the assumption of a dichotomy of the concept of law for the relationship between law and ethics? Anyone not wanting to permit the enforcement of extremely unjust rules or the inconsiderate exploitation of legal positions brings ethics, morals, morality or politics into play in conjunction with equity. Insofar as

[2] Karl Engisch, *Logische Studien zur Gesetzesanwendung* (3d ed.; 1963), p. 14 et seq. In substance, we find the idea of such simultaneity in Savigny, who discussed this subject under the heading "Methode der Römischen Juristen". Savigny, *Vom Beruf unsrer Zeit für Gesetzgebung und Rechtswissenschaft* (1814), p. 30 et seq. Unlike Engisch, Savigny began his "wandering" not with the "major premise" of the syllogism but with the "liveliest view" of the individual case.

equity does not remain "mute" but is "heard", the fields of law and ethics will overlap. At least, this is how Savigny understood it in his famous concept of law as a boundary or limit. Between the "circles" of law and ethics – Savigny spoke of morality – a sharp line must be drawn: in relations pertaining to ownership, formal law prevails as a matter of principle. Here "the rich man can cause the poor man to perish by refusing to support him".[3] Law and morality, however, are by no means just different; they are also connected. Law is capable of limiting the freedom secured by formal rationality, for example, by mitigating hardships or correcting injustices that are due to an exploitation of formal legal positions:

> Hence at the same time the relationship and the difference between law and morality comes to be understood. The law serves morality, not by performing its bidding but by securing the free development of its power indwelling in each individual will. The existence of law is however a self-dependent one, and hence there is no contradiction when in the individual case, the possibility of immoral exercise of a right actually existing, is asserted.[4]

[3] Savigny, *System des heutigen römischen Rechts* (1840), I, §56, p. 371. English translation: William Holloway, *System of the Modern Roman Law* (1867), available online.

[4] Savigny, *System des heutigen römischen Rechts,* note 3 above, §52, p. 332. There also, on the concept of right as a boundary: "The rule, by which those boundaries ant that free space [freye Raum] are determined is the law". Ibid., p. 332; English version: note 3 above, p. 269. The statement has more often been taken as evidence that Savigny must be read in a Kantian way because, like Kant, he derived all law from the moral freedom of each individual and thus argued merely in terms of individual ethics. Franz Wieacker, *Privatrechtsgeschichte der Neuzeit: Unter besonderer Berücksichtigung der deutschen Entwicklung* (2d ed.; 1967), p. 353. This interpretation fails to recognize that Savigny speaks not only of difference, but also of relationship, and therefore has no problem with including ethical elements in his concept of law as well (on the formal right of the rich, see the reference in note 3 above; on the requirement of mitigating hardships, see *System des heutigen römischen Rechts,* op. cit., §15, pp. 54-56). Since equity is (merely) a catch-all term and also includes utilitarian considerations of expediency (*ratio utilitatis*), the law would, according to Savigny, also be able to provide compensation for power imbalances. Less elaborated, but identical in essence, this dualism is also found in many other authors of the Romanist branch. It could indeed be said: the dualism constitutes almost the proprium of the concept of law

Thus, a plaintiff can appeal to formal legal positions in a lawsuit even if their enforcement would conflict with ethical imperatives or political maxims. This is because while law is autonomous, it is also not completely disconnected from the realms of material rationality. It is rather difficult to ascertain in which situations equity may be applied against formal rationality. Indeed, Leibniz already said that equity can only be determined *"difficillime generaliter"*.[5] Important considerations here are the situational character of equity, the circumstances of the individual case, extreme injustice, hardship, unreasonable aspects, exploitation of formal legal positions, abuse of rights, disproportionality, exceptions to rules, new cases, loopholes or the silent aspect of the law. At first glance, it might seem as if formal law stops where an exception (*exceptio*) is considered permissible for an individual case. But formal law continues to be valid even if it is not respected in a specific case because of ethical imperatives or political maxims.[6] It is not possible to

of the Historical School of Law. See Stephan Meder, "*Aequitas* und *ius strictum* in der Historischen Rechtsschule und Pandektistik", in Matthias Armgardt and Hubertus Busche (eds.), *Recht und Billigkeit* (2021). Savigny's complex ideas about the "relationship" of law and morality (*System des heutigen römischen Rechts*, op. cit., §52) cannot be discussed in more detail here, however.

[5] Gottfried Wilhelm Leibniz, *Elementa Juris Naturalis* (1669-1671), in Leibniz, *Sämtliche Schriften und Briefe. BAND 1: Sämtliche Schriften und Briefe (1663-1672)*, (2d ed.; 1990), Akademie-Ausgabe VI 1 p. 455. It has been repeatedly noted in the literature that "algorithm logic" could lead to depersonalization – to a disappearance of the subject in law (see the references in Frederik v. Harbou, "Abschied vom Einzelfall? - Perspektiven der Digitalisierung von Verwaltungsverfahren", *JuristenZeitung*, LXXV (2020), pp. 346, 348). It is true that a decision based on patterns and uniform features runs the risk of misjudging the individuality of cases and the special features that give a particular event its uniqueness. See also note 17 as well as chapter 9, at the end. It remains to be noted, however, that equity, to put it simply, is a collective term for "ethics" which, for instance in the name of sustainability, protects not only the individual or their subjective interest, but also the common good (see the example below in chapter 7).

[6] For details, see Okko Behrends, *Struktur und Wert* (1990), in Behrends, *Institut und Prinzip* (2004), I, pp. 55-89. On the legal philosophical foundations of the system of rule and exception, see Stephan Meder, *Der unbekannte Leibniz* (2018), pp. 77-83. It is understood that "rule" in the sense of formal rationality includes, in particular, freedom and equality (note 4 above: "der freye Raum"). Gierke disputed that freedom and equality can confer an unrestricted power of domination on the

provide a general answer to the question of whether formal or material elements take precedence. It may be assumed, however, that the "application" of formal law is supported by the assumption of its correctness. This assumption absolves those from responsibility who want to rely on it because they do not want to deduce or justify the values underlying the law. In cases where the application of formal law would lead to injustice, those that find themselves compelled to mitigate the hardships must present valid grounds why a deviation is a necessary exception in this case. The assumption thus dictates that the party seeking to contradict it bears a special burden of argument. If the formal law had no independent weight, no rank of its own, detailed reasoning in deviating cases would be superfluous. Imposing the burden of argument makes it more difficult to eliminate formal law, so that it still has a binding effect even where it is interrupted by considerations of equity.

The interplay between rule and exception can thus be specified as the rigor of formal law being mitigated in certain cases, being limited in its execution or enforcement, and at the same time being thought of as a continuing existence. The advantage of formal law is obvious. It is designed to be permanent, it conveys clarity, certainty, predictability and is, not least for this reason, associated with the subsumption automaton or mechanical application of the law. It is unnecessary to elaborate on details here; it suffices to say that Savigny's concept of law is not limited to formal law, but also includes ethical imperatives and political maxims. He conceptualized formal and material aspects of the law as an interplay where the paradoxical structures are explained

individual will. According to him, "it contradicts the deeper insight into the nature of things to establish the principle of equality in order to immediately eliminate it again by allowing a hundred exceptions. For either the principle is correct: then the exceptions are contrary to principle and press for elimination: or the exceptions are well founded: then the principle is an empty and harmful abstraction". Gierke, *Das deutsche Genossenschaftsrecht* (1873), II, p. 35. Gierke thus objected to the separation of rule and exception and seeks to dissolve this dualism of legal philosophy in a "material" monism. In this respect, he is correctly described as a pioneer of the notorious "internal theory" ("Innentheorie"; see chapter 7 below), to whom, in the words of Max Weber, "precisely the irrational, anti-formal element" was scientifically appealing (chapter 4).

on the basis of "difference" and "relationship". Kant's philosophical idealism, on the other hand, is based on an *a priori* concept of freedom, as already indicated. His concept of the law can only recognize "difference", that is, only the formal law, which is rigorously split off from morality. On the basis of a singular conception of law, Kant postulated precisely the type of formalization that the metaphor of the subsumption automaton, at least in its critical variants, seeks to make a caricature of. The formal perspective survives in the mainstream to this day, notwithstanding the teachings of the Historical School of Law, the doctrine of Free Law, the sociology of law, and various post-positivist theories. This is illustrated by the response of David Precht, the popular German philosopher and author, when asked in a recent interview whether all thought processes might one day be taken over by machines:

> When it comes to thinking, I'm skeptical, too, but where it concerns the law, you really only rarely need to think! In the end, the legal profession is nothing more than a large classification system that can be easily rattled through. And that already exists: Do you know 'Watson', the semantic search engine developed by IBM? A computer into which you can enter any normal legal question and then receive a printout of the expertise you need. Of course, there will still be lawyers who will handle complicated matters that require creative solutions. But the typical lawyer will, like a lot of other service providers, disappear[7]

[7] "Der Philosophie steht eine neue grosse Zeit bevor", Interview by Claudia Mäder with David Precht, *Neue Zürcher Zeitung*, 19 November 2016, p. 48. Another example could be the play "Terror" written by the trained lawyer, writer and playwright Ferdinand von Schierach, who also seeks to reduce "law" to its formal qualities. The play ran in theaters with great success and was broadcast as a television film by German public broadcaster ARD on 17 October 2016. The plot centers on the hijacking of a commercial airliner with 164 passengers that terrorists tried to take down over a soccer stadium filled with 70,000 spectators. The defendant is a German Army pilot who shot down the plane against the orders of his superior. The trial in the play centers on the question of whether an abstract principle could prevent the pilot from saving 70,000 lives by killing 164 passengers. The principle at issue here is human dignity, according to which every single life deserves absolute protection. According to the script, the pilot should have been convicted of murdering 164 people under the current German law. The fact that

Apart from the fact that Watson has not yet been used for legal decisions, the phrase "rattling through very easily" immediately suggests a mechanistic paradigm that is supposed to determine the legal order and all legal activity. If you look up the meaning of "rattern" (the word Precht uses in German is translated here as "rattling through") in the German dictionary, you will find illustrative examples: it is used in conjunction with "sewing machines, jackhammers, cars in the streets". Precht thus uses the image of machines, although he seems to have a rather older model in mind than Kantorowicz or Kafka. Kafka's apparatus, at least on the last and final level, works "completely silently and without the slightest whirring" when it is started. The mechanistic paradigm is, of course, to be applied only to the vast majority of supposedly clear-cut cases, the "lower jurisprudence" of the "run-of-the-mill lawyer". In the more remote spheres of "higher jurisprudence", the so-called "hard cases", there would still be a demand for "creative solutions". This picture of a hierarchical class society of cases based on complexity is, unfortunately, too good to be true. Any legally trained person who has had the opportunity to gain experience in the practical legal world knows that the simplest cases can pose almost insurmountable problems. Even where the legal system pushes the level of formalization to the extreme, for example regarding numbers or time periods, the real world

he saved 70,000 lives through his actions could not have been taken into account because of the formal nature of human dignity: for a sharp distinction would have to be made between law and ethics; only in ethics, but not in law, could a solution have been found for such situations of conflict. As much as this criticism of law may meet the expectations of the public, it is inaccurate. The legal system certainly allows exceptions to formal law via the principle of equity, here in the form of personal appropriateness, which has also been pointed out in legal academia. See Wolfgang Schild, *Verwirrende Rechtsbelehrung. Zu Ferdinand von Schierachs 'Terror'* (2016); Thomas Fischer, "'Terror' – Ferdinand von Schirach auf allen Kanälen", *Zeit Online*, 18 October 2016 (available online). Otherwise, the script correctly paid tribute to Kant's philosophy of law (from the point of view of a radical separation of law and ethics) (differently Fischer, op. cit., p. 5), but failed to recognize that, given its single-mindedness, it falls far short of the achievements of a tradition oriented towards Roman law. With the play "Terror", Ferdinand von Schierach joins that long line of authors who believe that law is first and foremost formal law. Then, "with law", one would indeed have to "think only rarely" and could "rattle through" the whole "system of order" like a machine "quite easily" (see also the notes on opinions from the field of literary studies in chapter 5 at note 10).

may nonetheless intrude on it to such a degree that its material rationality forces the judge to rule against the law.

THE COMPLEXITY OF "SIMPLE" CASES: MASS DESTRUCTION OF GOODS IN ONLINE RETAIL

One example of the ubiquitous intrusion of the real world into formal law and the insurmountable difficulties of supposedly simple cases is the consumer withdrawal period in online commerce. The right of withdrawal (§355 BGB) should be exceedingly easy to handle, as every "run-of-the-mill lawyer" should normally be able to realize their clients' claims quite easily. In accordance with the explicit will of the legislator, there are at least three reasons that consumers can withdraw from an online order. The right of withdrawal does not contain legal elements that need to be fulfilled, it does not require a specific reason, the motives of the consumer are completely irrelevant.[8] The consumer's right of withdrawal thus forms the pattern of a pure, strict, "formal" right, comparable to a regulation limiting a period or the age of majority. In contrast to indeterminate legal concepts or legal elements of a statute that provide room for equity, the judge's scope for discretion here tends toward zero.

A consequence of the right to withdrawal is that consumers act as if they want to examine the goods they have ordered, even though they know from the outset that they do not want to keep them. Examples include high-quality televisions ordered shortly before major sporting events, or wedding dresses ordered immediately before the wedding and then returned under the consumer's right of withdrawal. The costs of mass returns are immense. In addition, they cause considerable ecological damage and are beginning to have a negative impact on consumer prices. Thus, courts are increasingly confronted with the need to follow ethical imperatives and political maxims, such as sustainability or

[8] On the consumer's right of withdrawal, see, for example, Bürgerliches Gesetzbuch (BGB), §355(1), 4th sentence. For details, see Stephan Meder, "Das Verbraucherwiderrufsrecht", *juris PraxisReport Bank- und Kapitalmarktrecht*, VII (2018), note 1 (with further references).

climate protection, in order to allow exceptions to formal law in the interest of the common good. How can this need be accommodated? The answer is simple, but it does not fit into the picture that popular philosophers seem to have regarding the activity of a "run-of-the-mill lawyer": the need can be accommodated in the form of a decision *contra legem*!

In this context, it is worth recalling once again the dictum of the constitutional law expert Julius Hatschek cited above: according to the principle of separation of powers, German judges are "subsumption automatons": "If judges are to be more than mere applicators of the law, then they themselves become legislators! This is to be avoided at all costs".[9] German judges have often been criticized for paying too much tribute to such imperatives. One example is the controversy surrounding the doctrine of the so-called "objective interpretation", which allows judges to circumvent the separation of powers by claiming that their own decision is the decision of the legislature. Against this backdrop, it is not surprising that, following the example of Gnaeus Flavius, there have been repeated calls for the real motives to finally be stated in the reasoning of the decision. The separation of powers, however, often prevents judges from stating the true reasons, always assuming that they know them themselves, of course. This is because the truth, no matter of how "just" or "fair" the decision, might arouse the suspicion that judiciary wants to rebel against the law or even elevate itself to the position of legislator. "Civil law" does not envisage such a role for the judge. This is probably one reason why it has been repeatedly pointed out that reasoning of decisions is superior in "common law" countries.[10] A simple case of exercising the right of withdrawal in online commerce challenges the principle of a three-pronged division of powers and thus the foundations of our German understanding of democracy. Can a correction of the right of withdrawal, which is ultimately based on an European Union directive, be legitimate at all?

[9] Julius Hatschek, *Englisches Staatsrecht mit Berücksichtigung der für Schottland und Irland geltenden Sonderheiten: Die Verfassung* (1905), I, p. 157 (see also chapter 6, note 18).

[10] See also Oskar Hartwieg, *Tatsachen- und Normarbeit im Rechtsvergleich* (2003), pp. 73-74.

Caught between Scylla and Charybdis, the German Federal Court of Justice (BGH) has been searching for a remedy since its first decision on the limits of consumer withdrawal in online commerce (2005) and, as is to be expected in Europe, finds it in the written law. The court justifies the exception to the formal law thus: "The principle of performance in good faith, enshrined in §242 BGB, constitutes a limitation of substance immanent in all rights".[11] What does this mean? Are judges allowed to change the law at will on the basis of good faith or equity? So does it exist after all, the oft-invoked "limitless interpretation" or kadi justice? Anyone looking for an answer in the decisional reasoning is doomed to disappointment. The judiciary always limits itself to the same formula of the "immanent limitation of the content of all rights". Only the first judgment of 2005 contains a subtle reference, namely to the famous "Palandt" legal commentary. This refers to the controversial "internal theory" and names some older BGH judgments and some academic legal scholars who also follow this doctrine. The subtlety of this reference may be connected to the fact that the "internal theory" ("Innentheorie") was developed in the 1930s by Wolfgang Siebert, a leading jurist during the Nazi era.[12] It continues to be highly attractive for jurisprudence because it allows formal law to be dissolved at any time and without further justification, and the appearance of legitimacy to be lent to *contra legem* decisions.

[11] On current case law: Bundesgerichtshof, decision from 16 February 2005, *Neue Juristische Wochenschrift Rechtsprechungs-Report Zivilrecht*, IX (2005), p. 621; Bundesgerichtshof, decision from 12 July 2016, *Neue Juristische Wochenschrift*, XLVIII (2016), p. 3517 mn. 43; Oberlandesgericht Stuttgart, decision from 7 February 2017, *Zeitschrift für Bank- und Kapitalmarktrecht*, V (2017), p. 198 mn. 65 (in each case stating that only in individual cases can it be determined "which requirements result from this"). Regarding the first decision (16 February 2005, op.cit.). See also Otto Palandt, *Bürgerliches Gesetzbuch: BGB* (64th ed.; 2005), §242 mn. 38.

[12] On the internal theory ("Innentheorie"): Palandt, note 11 above, §242 mn. 38; *Entscheidungen des Bundesgerichtshofes in Zivilsachen*, XXX, p. 145; Hans Carl Nipperdey and Ludwig Enneccerus, *Allgemeiner Teil des Bürgerlichen Rechts* (15th ed.; 1960), §239 III (pp. 1439-1443). In essence: Wolfgang Siebert, *Verwirkung und Unzulässigkeit der Rechtsausübung* (1934); Siebert, "Die neueste grundsätzliche Entscheidung des Reichsgerichts über die Verwirkung", *Juristische Wochenschrift* (1937), pp. 2495 -2496. For details, see Hans-Peter Haferkamp, in *Historisch-Kritischer Kommentar zum BGB* (2007), II(1), §242 mn. 53 et seq.

During the National Socialist era, such legitimations were widespread. The background to this was the endeavor to resolve the outdated dualism of rule and exception into a monism of "materializations". Legal thought that originated in the nineteenth century and was discredited as formalistic, conceptually legalistic, literal, liberal, unsuitable for practice, Roman, un-German or foreign, was to give way to the new world view. The order of the day was to think of ways of destroying formal rationality by means of a "limitation of content imminent in all rights". The feared Nazi ideologist Roland Freisler, for example, saw the separation of judges and the law as an end that would only be reached when "the forces of renewal had worked their way out of being buried under the rubble of a liberal-individualist alternative-minded past".[13] The strong, nearly Herculean judge, celebrated by National Socialist jurisprudence turned out instead to be a small weakling that had, on order from above, to help the ideology succeed.

After the end of World War II, this kind of voice grew quieter, but there was still support for the merits of the internal theory: with good reason, the idea of a "limitation of content immanent in all rights" aimed to render the "rigid rules" of Roman jurisprudence relative and to dissolve the lines of difference that the Historical School of Law had drawn between formal and material law, on the basis that it would be an unacceptable contradiction if the law granted positions that could be restricted again in individual cases. Instead, formal law and the limits of how it was applied were to be merged into an inseparable unity. The limits of the right should therefore be determined out of the respective right itself: From its "ethical and social functions", it would follow "that an act of application that is contrary to purpose and function is no longer covered by the content of the right".[14]

[13] See the references in Lothar Gruchmann, *Justiz im Dritten Reich 1933-1940* (1988), p. 860. The freedoms that the internal theory grants the judges vis-à-vis the law are to be understood in this context (see also chapter 3 at note 12).

[14] Nipperdey, Enneccerus, note 12 above, p. 1440. It is therefore often emphasized that it does not correspond to liberal, but to "German legal thinking". Ibid., pp. 1440, 1442 et seq.; Siebert, "Die neueste

WEAKNESS OF THE INTERNAL THEORY – A PETITIO PRINCIPII

The problems of this view can be illustrated by the example of consumer withdrawal from above. According to the legislator's declared will, the right of withdrawal should be allowed to be exercised without specification of reasons. Thus, the law itself does not contain any restrictions or limits. The supporters of the internal theory must therefore concede that norms and statutes are usually silent about their "ethical functions", so that it remains ambiguous whether the use of the right is genuine or "only appears to be genuine". It is therefore up to the judge to determine "the limits" both *ex officio* and in the individual case. In doing so, they are aware that their doctrine deviates considerably not only from the premises of Roman law and Pandectics, but also from the BGB. Even the authors of the BGB deemed legal conceptual monism in the form of a general restriction of formal law to be objectionable because it would "replace the objective legal norm with the judge's feeling and blur the boundary between law and morality". These concerns would ultimately stem from the fact that the liberal views "prevailing around 1900 were not exactly favorable to the idea of a general restriction on the application of law".[15]

The internal theory thus eliminated the primacy of formal law and allowed the double step of rule and exception (*exceptio*) to merge into a singular, open consideration. This tears down the bastion that the presumption of individual self-determination erects against political appropriation and also breaks down the resistance that the requirement of its refutation generates. Thus, "freedom", along with formal law, runs the risk of losing all sense of scale. The judicial Hercules can put the "values" he considers "reasonable"

Entscheidung", note 12 above, p. 2495 et seq. "Liberal" may be understood here in a pejorative sense as criticism of formal rationality. In this context, it is worth recalling once again the Gierke passage cited above (note 6).

[15] For evidence, see Nipperdey, Enneccerus, note 12 above, p. 1440. Once again, it becomes clear that behind a supposedly "unlimited interpretation" is the political intention to dissolve the traditional legal order in order to pave the way for the "new state" and the "new worldview" (see also chapter 3 at note 12).

into the concept of freedom in order to draw them out again as justification. The procedure of rules and exceptions would then have been replaced by a *petitio principii.*[16] Max Weber would have seen in such a circular methodology a prime example example of an irrational formation of law.

SUMMARY

The BGH ruling on consumer withdrawal is to be supported without reservation. In times of climate change, scarcity of resources, and ecological catastrophes, one of the most noble tasks of jurisdiction is to counteract the unchecked mass destruction of goods. As already explained, there is both a single-tier of "formal" law and a single-tier of "material" law. Both types of legal conceptual monism are to be rejected: the formal single-tier approach, because it would open the door to extreme injustice, and the material single-tier approach, because it could help subjective arbitrariness and kadi justice to enter the legal order. As far as the internal theory is concerned, history has provided sufficient opportunity for it to be demonstrated how susceptible material unity is to ideology, and the time has come to finally declare it obsolete. Incidentally, the case law on consumer withdrawal also sheds light on the emergence of common law. It is worth recalling the statements of Bruno Schmidt who said that customary law would arise only if legal practitioners did not act as "subsumption automatons" and exceeded the limits of their competence.[17]

[16] For example, see Siebert, "Die neueste Entscheidung", note 12 above, p. 2495 et seq. (a "German-law" view of the contract, in which the "task of shaping it in the overall order" derives from the heteronomously determined "idea of community in legal transactions among the people"). See also Karl Larenz, "Der Vertrag als Gestaltungsmittel der völkischen Ordnung", in Larenz, *Vertrag und Unrecht* (1937), pp. 31-36 (criticizing the formal-legal approach of liberalism; contract as possibility of shaping and creating that can serve a specific purpose "from the outset" and is shaped by the "national order" ["völkische Ordnung"]); Franz Wieacker, "Der Stand der Rechtserneuerung auf dem Gebiet des bürgerlichen Rechts", in: Karl August Eckhardt (ed.), *Deutsche Rechtswissenschaft* (1937), pp. 15 and 23 (criticizing the "liberal-individualist theory of society", from which the "legal subject" emerged with the "power of will conferred for its own sake").

[17] Bruno Schmidt, *Das Gewohnheitsrecht als Form des Gemeinwillens* (1899), p. 15 (see also chapter 6 at note 18). The legitimacy of such a transgression again depends on the postulate of a twofold legal concept,

These conditions are undoubtedly fulfilled in the case of consumer withdrawal, because according to the clear will of the legislator, the motives for the withdrawal are not to be reviewed, that is, even actions that constitute an abuse of the law are permissible. Now, according to Schmidt, the government can either object to a judicial decision that deviates from the law or tacitly accept it. If the government remains silent and the *communis opinio* accepts the decision, new law arises in the form of customary law. In this sense, it is now accepted as a matter of customary law that courts in Germany can examine the motives for a consumer's

the attributes of which have been discussed in more detail in this chapter (see keywords "circumstances of the individual case", "hardship" or "abuse of rights", see, for example, chapter 7, note 5 above). Recently, it has been stated correctly that "general principles of justice in individual cases are difficult to derive from the constitution". Harbou, note 5 above, p. 348: "[...] At best, from the Basic Rights, which then require special treatment of persons if the application of *formal* rules [would mean] an *undue* burden" (Harbou, ibid., p. 348 – own translation, emphasis added; subsequent to Gabriele Britz, *Einzelfallgerechtigkeit versus Generalisierung* (2008), p. 12. From this perspective it is clear that the idea of justice in individual cases lies within a framework of conflict between *ius strictum* and *aequitas* (in the sense of a collective term that also encompasses the nature of the matter, proportionality, factual logic, or "life"). But do the Basic Rights, which are characterized in no small measure by their indefiniteness, truly capture the complex interrelationships of formal and material elements that are at the core of the concept of law? Would not the opposite be true for all who raise the argument of the principle of separation of powers? For the jurist in the continental European tradition, it is quite a temptation to refrain from explorations of the concept of law and to resolve the question of the legitimacy of "transgressions of limits" with a hermeneutic circle, that is, the simple reference to the constitution, legislation, or other "norms". Harbou emphasized that deciding whether the "application of *formal* rules" imposes an "*undue* burden" requires "elaborate substantive evaluations". But what are these evaluations? Do they only apply to public law or also to private law? And: how big is the effort? Do Harbou's comments aim at the justification effort that the supporters of the internal theory (see chapter 7 above) believe they can avoid? Do those comments deal with the effort that must be made by those who understand equity as a collective term for a kind of "ethics" that, as the "other side of law" (chapter 8), manages to refute the assumption of the application of "*formal* rules" in certain extraordinary cases. On the tensions between individual and social legal ethics, see Stephan Meder, "Zwischen strengem Formalismus und totaler Materialisierung", *Kritische Justiz*, LII (2019), p. 534. That second question, which is at the same time an answer, also raises awareness of the so-called "third-party effect of fundamental rights" and the distinction between "simple law" and constitutional law: the "elaborate material evaluations" have to be made where the problem arises (see chapter 7). Simple law can thus be difficult.

withdrawal. Despite all prophecies of doom: customary law is still capable of overriding statutory law!

The third, most obvious possibility, namely that the problem be regulated by governmental legislation, remained understandably unconsidered by Bruno Schmidt. He was aware that, despite the abundance of norms and regulations, it is rare for a legislator to take the initiative in such cases. For example, it took almost a century in German law before previously customarily recognized legal concepts, such as *culpa in contrahendo,* positive breach of contract, or cessation of the basis of the contract, found their way into statutory law. The particular appeal of the *contra legem* rulings on consumer withdrawal in online commerce now comes from the fact that the German Environment Ministry actually presented a draft statute intended to curb the mass destruction of goods.[18] Yet the focal point here is not the consequences of the problem of an unrestricted withdrawal right created by the legislature itself, but rather the online retailers, who are to be prohibited from destroying the returns en masse. Whether there is any merit in this endeavor can be left open to debate. From the perspective of legal source theory, it is rather more interesting to ask: what are the limits of a subsumption machine? How can valuations that the judiciary finds itself compelled to make generate new law?

The recent statute drafted by the German Ministry for the Environment to prevent the destruction of goods suggests tacit acceptance of the customary law on consumer withdrawal. After all, anyone professing to want to put a stop to mass destruction of goods will be wary of using the separation of powers as a reason to contradict decisions that strive for the same goal. From here, another problem emerges that, as far as can be seen, has not yet been addressed in the literature on legal tech: The notion of "value judgment" must be understood in a broad sense, with even the seemingly simplest cases in mind. The function certainly cannot be only to alleviate the hardships encountered in the legal process or

[18] See the report, "Regierung will massenhafte Warenvernichtung stoppen", *Die Zeit,* 12 February 2020, p. 12 (the report of course is unaware of the problem that the unrestricted withdrawal imposed by the legislature poses for legal practice).

to plug gaps in the legal system. Value judgments can also lead to adaptations of existing law in response to changing social conditions and to the correction of iniquitous choices by the legislature by means of making changes in existing law and creating new law. Such statements will, however, be sought in vain in the grounds for decisions of the highest courts in Germany. For they counteract the idea of the subsumption automaton and must, as Hatschek has pointed out – not without irony – "be avoided at all costs".

Chapter 7 From Subsumption Automaton to Algocracy

The first legal machine age began, as explained above, a good century before the Industrial Revolution, around the mid-seventeenth century. A famous example illustrating the constitutional philosophical premises of rationalism under the Law of Reason is Hobbes's overpowering automaton, *Leviathan*. This automaton, in the guise of an "artificial man", operates on a *tabula rasa* and can decide on anything and everything. According to the political metaphor of the State as a machine, the most noble task of the sovereign is to "prescribe" the laws according to his will as precisely, accurately, and in as much detail as possible, in order to confine the judge to the letter and wording of a text. Savigny, Puchta, and many others took up arms against the formal rationality of decision-making in political voluntarism at the beginning of the nineteenth century, only to become targets of criticism soon thereafter. That the misinterpretations of "jurisprudence of concepts" had a dominating effect in the last century and persist in essence today has already been explained. The idea of the subsumption automaton received new impetus about fifty years ago, when the first signs of a second age of the legal machine became noticeable. Its characteristics are currently the subject of vigorous and intense discussion again under labels such as autonomous technical systems and legal technology.

THE SUBSUMPTION AUTOMATON 1.0 – FIRST PROGRAMS FOR THE FORMALIZATION OF LEGAL DECISION-MAKING RATIONALITY

In the late 1960s and early 1970s, a group of legal scholars, logicians, computer scientists, and linguists attempted to establish the foundations for automated analysis of the interpretation of legislative texts. The same advantages of a technical solution to the problem are being asserted today: facilitating the work of the judiciary, increasing the speed and cost-effectiveness of judgments, and excluding the private opinions of decision-makers. The goal was to develop programs for formalizing legal propositions and for deriving subsumptions from a formal logical comparison of major and minor premises on the basis of a narrow, neopositivist concept of science and academia, which recognizes only those research methods that are highly formalized and developed from algorithms derived from logics.[1] As far as terminology is concerned, it is noticeable that previously frowned-upon terms such as mechanical or automatic subsumption, as well as logic, deduction, and mathematics, could now be used impartially and without reservations even in circles well-grounded in legal theory. The decision-making automaton seems to have lost its pejorative connotations in the last third of the twentieth century, at least among a considerable number of legal scholars: it came to be seen no longer as an embarrassment, but, as had been true during the first legal machine age, as progress and a desirable goal. In retrospect, however, a perplexingly unreflective concept of subsumption emerged, which conflated intuitive valuations or valuations hidden in subjective preconceptions as well as logical calculations.[2]

[1] The era of Subsumption Automaton 1.0 is characterized by an increased interest in methodological and legal theoretical issues. Thus, contemporary papers and studies frequently take up the topic of the alleged nineteenth century "jurisprudence of concepts" and its relation to the jurisprudence of interests or values. Because there is often a lack of legal historical expertise, it is the standard to use the polemics of Jhering and Kantorowicz, as postulated and carried forward by Wieacker, Larenz, Canaris, and countless other authors in the second half of the twentieth century. See the references in Thomas Jandach, *Juristische Expertensysteme: Methodische Grundlagen ihrer Entwicklung* (1993), pp. 105-109; Svenja Lena Gräwe, *Die Entstehung der Rechtsinformatik. Wissenschaftsgeschichtliche und -theoretische Analyse einer Querschnittsdisziplin* (2011), pp. 183-185. Thus, surprisingly, the still fresh field of legal computer science is one area of jurisprudence in which "jurisprudence of concepts" is most frequently mentioned. An early critical discussion of the accusation of positivism against a formal decision rationality can be found in Wolfgang Kilian, *Juristische Entscheidung und elektronische Datenverarbeitung. Methodenorientierte Vorstudie* (1974), pp. 22-24. On the contemporary discussion of legal machines and decision theory, see also the work of Wieacker, chapter 3 at notes 24 to 27.

[2] The project is documented in Dieter Rave, Hans Brinckmann, and Klaus Grimmer (eds.), *Paraphrasen juristischer Texte. Referate und Protokolle der Arbeitstagung im Deutschen Rechenzentrum Darmstadt, 24.-26. Juni 1971* (1971). The above account is essentially based on

This is where the opponents of the first efforts to formalize decision rationality come in. Here one must recall some objections raised by the brothers Hubert L. and Stuart E. Dreyfuß in 1986. Eighty years after the publication of Kantorowicz, "Kampf um die Rechtswissenschaft", they also referred to a "thinking machine", starting with the subtitle of their widely discussed book on the limits of information-technological progress.[3] In it, they argue that all attempts to replicate the natural ability to speak on a computer are doomed to failure, for everyday human competences are based not on norms but on intuition as a form of bodily understanding. This kind of knowledge can generally not be reconstructed with rules. Therefore, humans must necessarily maintain a lead over computers. The dominant thesis, hotly debated today, was that some specific human tasks could not be performed by "thinking machines" simply because these operate differently from human beings. On the other side were those who thought that computers really were as powerful as the visionaries of information technology claimed. This is precisely why certain decisions should not be left to computers under any circumstances, even if they were to acquire the ability to make such decisions one day. Undeterred by such

Dietrich Busse, *Juristische Semantik. Grundfragen der juristischen Interpretationstheorie in sprachwissenschaftlicher Sicht* (1993), pp. 140-161. See also Bernd Jeand'Heur, "Die neuere Fachsprache der juristischen Wissenschaft seit der Mitte des 19. Jahrhunderts unter besonderer Berücksichtigung von Verfassungsrecht und Rechtsmethodik", in Hugo Steger and Herbert Ernst Wiegand (eds.), *Handbücher zur Sprach- und Kommunikationswissenschaft* (1998), XIV(1), p. 1294; Dietrich Busse, "Textlinguistik und Rechtswissenschaft", in Klaus Brinker, Gerd Antos, Wolfgang Heinemann, and Sven Frederik Sager (eds.), *Text- und Gesprächslinguistik, 1st half vol. Handbücher zur Sprach- und Kommunikationswissenschaft* (2000), XVI(1), pp. 804-807; Friedemann Vogel, "Rechtslinguistik: Bestimmung einer Fachrichtung", in Ekkehard Felder and Friedemann Vogel (eds.), *Handbuch Sprache im Recht* (2017), pp. 215, 223. Marc Queudot and Marie-Jean Meurs traced the scientific attempts of applying quantitative methods to legal decision-making (*Jurimetrics*) back to 1963. See "Artificial Intelligence and Predictive Justice: Limitations and Perspectives", in Malek Mouhoub, et al. (eds.), *Recent Trends and Future Technology in Applied Intelligence* (2018), p. 889.

[3] Hubert L. Dreyfuß and Stuart E. Dreyfuß, *Künstliche Intelligenz. Von den Grenzen der Denkmaschine und dem Wert der Intuition* (1987); Joseph Weizenbaum, *Die Macht der Computer und die Ohnmacht der Vernunft* (1976).

reservations, many authors continued to pin their hopes on the subsumption automaton, believing that computerized application of the law could ensure that decision-making becomes less costly and more independent.[4]

In order to exclude normatively undesirable individual preferences or prejudices, early attempts were made to program automata in such a way that they operate only within decision trees. "Decision trees" are so appealing to European jurisprudence because their diagrams offer a structure that is consistent with a judicial syllogism in many respects: decision trees are vertically structured and operate on the basis of predefined rules. As each path is based on the so-called "*if-then*" rule, logical deductions can be made and outcomes derived. From a legal point of view, the branch ends show the factual requirements of statutory norms, the application of which must be unambiguously either affirmed or denied. Under the premises of law-abiding application of law, such a binary opposition must be self-evident, as rules expressed in the factual elements of a statutory norm are often oriented towards an "if-then" scheme, that is, a conditional program, according to which the legal consequence in a specific case only occurs if all normative prerequisites are actually fulfilled.[5]

[4] On the discussion of automated subsumption in the 1980s and 1990s, see Peter Gerathewohl, *Erschliessung unbestimmter Rechtsbegriffe mit Hilfe des Computers* (1987); Manfred Weihermüller, "Künftiges Informationsmanagement von Juristen", in Carl-Eugen Eberle (ed.), *Informationstechnik in der Juristenausbildung* (1989), pp. 192-204; Heiner Hastedt, *Aufklärung und Technik. Grundprobleme einer Ethik der Technik* (1991), especially p. 69 et seq; Jandach, note 1 above; Hans Kudlich, "Information als Herausforderung und Informatik als Hilfsmittel für die Rechtsanwendung im Straf- und Strafprozessrecht", in Jürgen Taeger and Irini Vassilaki (eds.), *Rechtsinformatik und Informationsrecht im Spannungsfeld von Recht, Informatik und Ökonomie* (2009), pp. 13-23 (especially p. 19); Gräwe, note 1 above.

[5] For Niklas Luhmann, for example, the law of a modern constitutional state seemed virtually predestined for automation, because both had the same basic structure with the Conditional Scheme. See Luhmann, *Recht und Automation in der öffentlichen Verwaltung* (1966), pp. 35, 43 et seq: "The program instructions" concern "acts of choice between two possibilities each, the decision of which depends in each case on predetermined conditions"). From here it is a small step to Luhmann's later formulated assumption that the validity of law is based on a binary coding of right and wrong (critically, Stephan Meder, *Schuld, Zufall, Risiko* (1993), pp. 265-269). A good overview of the functioning of decision-trees can

This judicial syllogism constitutes the prime example of subsumption carried out in the context of conditional programs. That is not to say that there are not also conclusion procedures that go beyond a simple judicial-syllogistic reconstruction of the subsumption. As far as tree structures come into question, however, considerations and evaluations take a back seat to "calculating using the law". The formalization of decision-making rationality brought about by tree structures harmonizes with a legal education which is concentrated, in Germany at least, on the more traditional forms of vertical rule creation, on laws, regulations and administrative acts, that is, ultimately on requirements and prohibitions.

That this kind of "rationality" is based on a naive notion of what happens when humans make judgments has often been pointed out. Every jurist who has had the opportunity to gather practical experience knows that legal questions can only rarely be decided on the basis of conditional programs. The "if-then" pattern therefore shows up the limits of rule-based software and of decision trees. "Calculating with the law" is difficult in tree structures because the requirements of a statutory law are often undefined and legal terms can be worded openly, so that the process of finding the law is not vertical but horizontal. Additionally, legal language often allows for multiple possible interpretations and legal decisions themselves require consideration of "material" factors that lie beyond the written norms, even in seemingly straightforward cases. For these reasons, a second variety of automatic subsumption has recently joined the rule-

be found in Christoph Beierle and Gabriele Kern-Isberner, *Methoden wissensbasierter Systeme. Grundlagen, Algorithmen, Anwendungen* (6th ed.; 2019), pp. 106-116; Wolfgang Ertel, *Grundkurs Künstliche Intelligenz* (4th ed.; 2016), pp. 217-219, 308 et seq; Brijain R. Patel and Kushik K. Rana, "A Survey on Decision Tree Algorithm. For Classification", *International Journal of Engineering Development and Research*, II (2014), pp. 1-5; Vladan Vuckovic and Djordje Vidanovic, *A New Approach to Draw Detection by Move Repetition in Computer Chess Programming* (2014) (available online). Binary opposition plays an important role in current intelligent programs (see chapter 8 below). For example, judicial decisions are categorized into two categories when entered into a database, namely, if a case was successful or if it was dismissed. See Rhuan Barros, et al., "Case Law Analysis with Machine Learnig in Brazilian Court", in Malek Mouhoub, et al., note 2 above, p. 866; Queudot and Meurs, note 2 above, p. 893.

governed software, namely decision-making with the help of "adaptive" computer systems.

THE SUBSUMPTION AUTOMATON 2.0 - ARTIFICIAL INTELLIGENCE AND "LIFE"

The fact that computers can now compose pieces of music and are now superior to human players in checkers, chess, and Go has given new impetus to the discussions of whether legal decisions can also be made using automata. Unlike decisions trees, legal artificial intelligence no longer works primarily on the basis of predefined rules, but with large amounts of data in the form of legal facts, case law, legal texts, commentary literature, judgment reviews, or other sources, which are transformed into mathematical equations and examined according to their numerical frequency in relation to a specific legal question. Such systems do not formulate higher-level theories that could structure a subject area or a topic in the form of general propositions. Instead they look for correlations between given data points and develop suppositions and projections about the plausibility of patterns using probability and statistics.

A machine is said to have artificial intelligence if it is "capable of learning" and, after the learning phase, can process new, as yet unknown data in such a way that the output becomes independent of the input.[6] The lack of determination of intelligent systems, also called "emergence", has the consequence that individual steps can

[6] In machine learning, algorithms build a statistical model based on training data. They do not simply memorize rules or examples but recognize patterns and regularities in the learning data. In this way the system can recognize unknown data via a learning transfer – or fail to learn unknown data. Specifically concerning legal decisions, a large number of judgments are divided into individual main categories (see note 5 above) and according to differentiated features. An examination follows regarding how often which combination of features results into which legal consequence. If a combination of features relative to their absolute frequency results in a specific legal consequence in the majority of cases, the system learns this general rule that this combination of features leads to this legal consequence. On the "learning ability" of intelligent systems, see: Ulrich Eberl, "Was ist künstliche Intelligenz – was kann sie leisten?", *Aus Politik und Zeitgeschichte*, LXVIII (2018), p. 11 et seq.; Thomas Wischmeyer, "Regulierung intelligenter Systeme", *Archiv des öffentlichen Rechts*, CXLIII (2018), pp. 11-14; Ertel, note 5 above, p. 195; Felix Stalder, *Kultur der Digitalität* (2nd ed.; 2016), pp. 177-181.

no longer be reconstructed if they arouse suspicion, meaning that the decision can only be understood or predicted with limitations, if at all. It is, to adopt a word frequently used in this context, "opaque" whether the program merely identifies and reproduces existing patterns or "adds" something – and thus produces "new" law (the adjective "new" admittedly acquires its own connotation in the realm of artificial intelligence.) Intelligent systems can certainly "evaluate" or "weigh". However, they work on the basis of predefined data. The information they use and the results they produce are not based on immediate observation of facts or direct observation of hitherto unknown phenomena, but on evaluations that have already been made and cases that have been decided in the past. This creates a lack of transparency along with terrifying visions based on a fear that systems will operate in an algocracy and that the decisions of these systems will ultimately be inaccessible to human reason and understanding.[7]

Artificial intelligence can process formally determined rules and can detect patterns in the form of general statements, predictions or decisions using standards of frequency and probability. The question is, however, can the algorithm analyze, interpret, or understand the meaning of texts? The issue is interdisciplinary in character, involving linguistics as well as philosophy and legal theory. Is there an objective meaning of texts, particularly laws and other legal texts? The "linguistic turn" would lead to a negative answer to this question. Modern linguistics denies that language is a transparent medium to grasp that what we call reality or life. It assumes that all human cognition is "structured" by language and that reality beyond language is either non-existent or at least inaccessible. At this point, a connection

[7] John Danaher, "The Threat of Algocracy: Reality, Resistance and Accomodation", *Philosophy & Technology*, XXIX (2016), pp. 245-268; Jörn Erbguth, "Juristische Entscheidungen nach maschinellem Bauchgefühl", *Deutsche Richterzeitung*, 2018, pp. 130-131; Sebastian Unger, "Demokratische Herrschaft und künstliche Intelligenz", in Unger and Antje von Ungern-Sternberg (eds.), *Demokratie und künstliche Intelligenz* (2019), pp. 113-128. Frederik von Harbou, Abschied vom Einzelfall? – Perspektiven der Digitalisierung von Verwaltungsverfahren, *JuristenZeitung*, LXXV (2020), p. 345 („nicht selten bleiben die Zwischenschritte […] im Dunkel"). [not infrequently, the intermediate steps [...] remain in the dark].

with the Copernican turn, initiated by Kant, arises. The parallel to modern linguistics lies in the way that Kant gave up describing reality by relegating the "thing-in-itself" to the realm of transcendence. After the Copernican turn, he began to concentrate his research on the conditions of knowledge and, as is well known, he found it not in things, reality, actuality, world or "life", but in the structures of reason.

Those who question whether software is able to understand a text by processing even such a large amount of data must in turn face the question: is a human being able to do the same? Modern linguistics answers this question in the negative. This is because linguistics believes that no semantic meaning can be held in the text itself, but rather that the meaning is "first 'constructed' by the readers themselves".[8] Accordingly, there can be no objective understanding of the text. So, is the common ground shared between human beings and computers their ability to understand texts only in an approximate manner, if at all, and the existence of reality only in the constructions of their reason, language, or operations? Before attempting an answer to this, it is worth adding a comment regarding the connection with the formalism criticisms made by Jhering, Kantorowicz, and other authors at the turn of the twentieth century.

CONNECTION WITH THE LEGAL CRITICISM OF JHERING AND KANTOROWICZ

Jhering described in dialog-form Kant's transcendental philosophy according to which "the world that you deem to have perceived" exists only as "imagination" and in the shape of "forms of your subjective view." According to modern linguistics, these "forms of your subjective view" would have to be exchanged or supplemented by "forms of your linguistic constructions". The legal solutions that arise on the basis "do not agree with life, they require a world for themselves, in which they exist only for themselves and on their own, far from any contact with life".[9] Jhering

[8] See Axel Adrian, "Der Richterautomat ist möglich - Semantik ist nur eine Illusion", *Rechtstheorie*, XLVIII (2017), p. 84.

[9] See Chapter 2, at note 5 to 7.

complains here that Kant's transcendental philosophy reduces jurisprudence to a purely formal discipline that has lost any connection with social reality – and thus with "life". In fact, Kant holds that all actions in the legal field realize a rule of reason, the object of which "is not encountered at all apart from as a concept". As explained, the problem of Kant's philosophy of law is that it recognizes only the formal side of jurisprudence and seeks to suppress elements of material rationality as much as possible.[10] From the assumption of a constructed reality, then, we come full circle to a criticism of the law that was drafted more than a century ago.

From today's point of view, this observation raises two questions. First, whether there is a "life" beyond rational or linguistic forms at all? Second, if this is to be rejected: can we be indifferent to the question of whether a human or a machine interprets, because there is no objective understanding of texts and no reality beyond "forms" and linguistic "constructions" anyway? In jurisprudence there are voices that, looking at the results of modern linguistic philosophy, tend to answer this second question in the affirmative: "If a software evaluates differently than a human being, is that necessarily worse?"[11] Since the devotees of the "linguistic turn" are advancing in years and the philosophy of legal artificial intelligence is still in its infancy, it is no easy task to make concrete statements about the differences between human and machine interpretation, but perhaps these questions should at least be considered in an effort to formulate a few theses.

[10] Immanuel Kant, *Kritik der reinen Vernunft* (2d ed.; 1787), B 594, 506 (on this in more detail in chapter 2 at note 6; chapter 7 at note 7).

[11] Martin Fries, *Legal Tech, Lecture Slides* (2018), Unit 3 Künstliche juristische Intelligenz, p. 8 (available online). Luhmann said that it is irrelevant for the logical consistency and accuracy of a legal decision if decision programs are processed by the human brain or by machines. Luhmann, note 5 above, p. 46 f.: "In the final analysis, there are no rational reasons to prefer human performance to machine performance" ["Aufs letzte gesehen ... vorzuziehen] (op. cit., p. 60).

WHAT IS THE DIFFERENCE BETWEEN CHESS AND THE LAW?

Intelligent systems show to human beings patterns that they would otherwise never see or would recognize much more slowly. It is therefore understandable that every new "super-software" is met with admiration when it is released and is sometimes even credited with superhuman abilities. Machine reasoning is, however, limited, as a computer can only convey patterns generated on the basis of data provided. Chess software, chess engines, endgame or opening databases may exist which can astound any chess grandmaster. However, according to Philipp Slusallek from the German Research Center for Artificial Intelligence in Saarbrücken, these capabilities represent only a small slice of "all human capabilities": "Human capabilities are clearly dramatically broader, more general and more flexible than any computer will be in the foreseeable future".[12] Do these capabilities have to be dramatically broader, more general, and more flexible to judge a legal case?

What are the differences between chess and the law? Simply stated, chess is based on a closed order, the law on an open order. Chess is structured formally by strict rules that allow no exceptions. All chess pieces must be moved in a certain way depending on their type. A chess move must always be parried, the king can never be exposed to a threat, and the "touch-move"-rule means that it is essential to move a piece touched by the player who has the move. In addition to these examples, there are other rules that guarantee the match runs smoothly, and all have in common a lack of scope for consideration of mitigating circumstances. Chess

[12] Cited according to Norbert Lossau, "Diese Super-Software bringt sich übermenschliche Leistungen bei", *Welt*, 18 October 2017 (available online). "Chess has always been considered the appropriate area to work on in order to prove the capabilities of an artificial intelligence. Initially, it was believed that the same results could be obtained for language, such as fluency in English. However, this has proven to be a case of academic naiveté. To this day, there is no artificial system on the horizon that can come close to mastering English or any other language. The reason for this difference is seen in the fact that compared to language, chess presents a more closed problem area". Compare Heinz Mühlenbein, "Grenzen der künstlichen Intelligenz - Ein Plädoyer für Bescheidenheit", *Künstliche Intelligenz*, IX (1995), pp. 9 -11.

rules therefore have an immanent character; they cannot be limited, extended, or even corrected by external influences. Those who focus on the formal qualities of the law and understand it as a sum of immanent rules, reducing it to a closed system, comprehend the law as a kind of chess. This is the view of rationalist-era authors who believed they could eliminate external influences on the law, potentially in form of equity or interpretation, to the maximum extent. Despite all the criticism of formalism, this point of view has not been overcome yet. It lives on *mutatis mutandis* in the ubiquitous methodologies of faithful application of law and in popular conceptions of law.

We need only recall the remarks of the philosopher David Precht cited earlier that law is "nothing more than a large system of order that can be rattled through quite easily". The assertion that law is ultimately formal is, however, widespread not only among lay persons but even among legal professionals.[13] It also accords with an understanding of legal education that places an emphasis on elements of vertical norm-setting, on laws and regulations, and on commands and prohibitions. Similarly, the Subsumption Automaton 2.0 has already been confronted with formalist criticism, when the question is raised of whether, in view of the receptive structure of algorithmic selection, legal tech should not be interpreted as a new trend, towards a digital neo-positivism, for example.[14]

More complex post-positivist concepts of methodology may have to be adopted soon: the more closed a system presents itself as, the easier its rules can be comprehended according to the standards of formal rationality in decision making. The thesis would then be: we will experience a renaissance of legal formalism, and criticism of the jurisprudence of concepts will be quietly shelved. It will be replaced by an idea of jurisprudence as a closed system

[13] In this context, there is the idea, already formulated in the era of the Law of Reason, that the concept of law is reserved for norms of governmental origin. See the evidence on the current discussion and the problem of being able to correspond to transnational norm-buildings on this basis in Stephan Meder, *Doppelte Körper im Recht* (2015), p. 1.

[14] Wolfgang Hoffmann-Riem, "Verhaltenssteuerung durch Algorithmen", *Archiv des öffentlichen Rechts*, CXLII (2017), p. 17.

of order that can be "easily rattled through" in accordance with the standards of faithful application of the law. From here, it is but a small step to the unshakable conviction that legal professionals can soon be replaced with Artificial Intelligence.

Even under the premises of neo-positivism and formal law, differences from chess can be identified; in law the number of rules is considerably larger and legal language shows a fundamental openness to interpretation that would quickly bring the flow of a chess match to a standstill. Apart from that, however, the statement could stand: law and chess consist of an aggregate of rules that must as far as possible be undisturbed by factors that lie outside the system.

THE OTHER SIDE OF LAW: SITUATIONAL OPENNESS TO THE WORLD

As explained above, a monism of legal philosophy cannot do justice to the complexity of jurisprudence. In addition to "formal rationality", the law also has, to use Max Weber's term, a "material rationality". This means that, under certain circumstances, ethical imperatives, political maxims, or utilitarian considerations of expediency can affect the "system" from the outside and can augment it, correct it, or even derogate from some of its features. Instead of "the outside" or "the external", concepts of epistemology or scientific theory could also be brought into play, namely reality, actuality, the world, and "life". All of these designate that second element which distinguishes material rationality from merely formal rationality.

The consumer's right of withdrawal in online commerce was mentioned above as an example of an area in which formal elements are highly developed. And even as consumers availed themselves of this right on a massive scale, indeed shamelessly exploited it to their advantage, the general public began a debate about sustainability, scarcity of resources, climate change, piles of waste, throwaway societies, the waste of rare earths, and similar topics. The first German supreme court decisions on the application of equity to consumer's right of withdrawal marks the point at which an external force – reality, society, or "life" - breaks the habit of a formal construction - the right of withdrawal

- which, according to the will of the legislator, can be exercised without preconditions, thereby helping certain political maxims, ethical imperatives, or considerations of expedience to take hold.

This point of view sheds light on the statement that despite the almost infinite variations of the game and the sheer size of the game tree, playing chess calls upon only a "minimal section of human abilities". Limited abilities suffice because a board game, even with maximum game complexity, has no use for the degree of openness that dealing with uncertainty about the state of the world requires. Under the premises of a dichotomy in the concept of law, therefore, intrusions by the world into formal rationality must be expected at any time. But what does "world" mean? It has been doubted that reason or language are adequate means for grasping reality. Do we not live in a world filtered and constructed by media? Linguists, transcendentalist philosophers and postmodernists of various provenances would probably see it this way. They might also add that the filter works better in artificial intelligence because here the information must be translated into symbolic elements, and realities which have already been filtered thus must be further reduced to mathematical signs.

The application of artificial intelligence would therefore lead to the multiplication of filters, and this would dramatically increase distance from "reality". In addition, as is well known, machines possess no biological body. They "live" in a different "world" than humans and are thus unable to share many human experiences. It is probably for this reason that no machine has been able to reproduce human thought processes. The computer programs for checkers, chess, or Go work differently than human intelligence. More than that, human beings understand their own ways of thinking, if at all, only insufficiently, and so it has not yet been possible to describe the game play of a chess grandmaster in the form of algorithms. The latest "super-software" may meet with great admiration, but it has not been modeled on the imitation of human intelligence. The decisions reached in an algocracy would therefore be inaccessible or "opaque" to human understanding because they are not based on human thought processes. This flaw particularly affects legal reasoning and the content of the reasons in a court decision, and ultimately that decision's legitimacy. As long as it is unclear what the system adds, only the sentence "*auctoritas non veritas facit legem*" remains. Even the often claimed "intelligence" and "learning ability" of the systems cannot help overcome the risks of political decisionism or totalitarian rule. To claim otherwise trivializes human intelligence and displays naive anthropomorphism.

THE NEED FOR HUMAN CONTROL

Artificial intelligence can outperform human beings in many areas, as we have seen. However, the areas in which legal tech is applied are various and constantly changing. Online dispute resolution, smart contracts, legal robots, or legal generators such as deadline and fee calculators, which seemed utopian just a few years ago, are almost the norm today.[15] In addition, there are automata that operate at the edges of the legal system to eliminate blank areas on the legal map, such as disputes over minor sums that fall outside the scope of the law because enforcing claims entails to considerable risk in the form of litigation costs. For example, the high legal fees involved made it rarely worthwhile for rail or airline passengers to pursue legal claims in the event of delays.[16] Myright, Flightright, or Bahn-Buddy have developed business models on the basis of the volume of such cases, even if the field still requires legal theoretical exploration. Is this a hitherto unknown form of self-regulation, governance, and private lawmaking? Are such "refreshing alternatives to conventional legal practice"

[15] For the current use of digital technologies, see Oliver Raabe et al., *Recht ex machina* (2012); Jens Wagner, "Legal Tech und Legal Robots in Unternehmen und den diese beratenden Kanzleien", *Betriebs-Berater*, XVII (2017), pp. 898-905; Anika Klafki, et al. (eds.), *Digitalisierung und Recht* (2017); David Jost and Johann Kempe, "E-Justice in Deutschland. Eine Bestandsaufnahme zur Digitalisierung der Justiz", *Neue Juristische Wochenschrift*, XXXVIII (2017), pp. 2705-2708.

[16] Ulrike Barth, "Legal Tech in Deutschland – zwischen Buzz Word und Anwaltsschreck", in Markus Hartung, Micha-Manuel Bues and Gernot Halbleib (eds.), *Legal Tech. Die Digitalisierung des Rechtsmarktes* (2018), p. 48 et seq.; Ralf B. Abel, "Automatisierte Entscheidungen im Einzelfall gem. Art. 22 DS-GVO", *Zeitschrift für Datenschutz*, VII (2018), p. 306; Christian Wolf, "Der Schlüssel zu einem effizienten Zivilprozessrecht", *Zeitschrift für Rechtspolitik*, VI (2018), p. 185.

(Flightright) sources of new law which would not exist without the technical applications?

To date, lawyers must still appear in court whenever no solution can be found on the basis of standardized work. Low amounts of money also play an important role in the insurance industry, and algorithms almost universally decide on claims if they are below a specified insured amount. Where the circumstances of the claim and the profile of the insured person show no abnormalities, the payment is issued automatically without further checks. Questions of legitimacy are not apparent as the insurance company alone bears the risk of an incorrect decision.[17]

That said, a computer may not reject a claim from the insured party automatically. Any rejections are to be left to a claims agent who will check whether the business relationship with the client has existed for a longer period of time, whether considerations of equity or goodwill come into play, and whether a payment made without legal grounds appears to be justified by way of exception. At this point, the openness of the legal system comes into play once again, and serves as a reminder of the differences between human and artificial intelligence. Accordingly, a verification of the automated decision will always be necessary if a decision is likely to be made to the detriment of the person concerned. Once again, the reason is that the results of artificial intelligence are not a replica of human thought processes. There is good reason to insist that the highest standards must be applied to the supervision by humans. Mere plausibility checks are not sufficient. The formal rationality of decisions made in unsettled matters is not sufficient: the human beings involved must be able at all times to question by independent means decisions made by automata.[18]

[17] Under such premises, it seems legitimate if the algorithm (in the context of self-regulation and private lawmaking) does not have to be disclosed. The topic of "subsumption automata in the insurance industry" has, as far as can be seen, not yet been discussed in depth in academia. Thanks go to Alexander Djazayeri for valuable suggestions.

[18] Albrecht von Graevenitz, "'Zwei mal Zwei ist Grün' – Mensch und KI im Vergleich", *Zeitschrift für Rechtspolitik*, VIII (2018), p. 240; Ariane Berger, "Der automatisierte Verwaltungsakt", *Neue Zeitschrift*

OUTLOOK

Formal rationality in decision-making is hardly suited to solving problems in open systems like the law. It would therefore be better to demand in place of an artificial "machine" a natural one which, like the brain or consciousness, would ideally be able to access all human capabilities at any time and to perceive them directly. It is not without reason that warnings against underestimating the difference between the natural and the artificial have recently been repeated in the context of the cautionary tale of the "Human Brain Project", for which the European Commission provided the colossal sum of one billion Euro as third-party funding. The task of the project leaders and the team was simply to replicate the human brain in a computer. The achievement of that extraordinary goal would entail the kind of real "breakthrough" so often expected in tenders for third-party funding projects.[19] However, we humans do not yet understand the workings of the brain of a threadworm consisting of only three hundred neurons, and so replicating the human brain with its hundreds of billions of neurons was an unattainable goal from the outset. As we have seen, neither the human brain nor human consciousness can be reproduced digitally as they are not limited to the ability to calculate. The project was closed down when experts warned of the astounding waste of funding.

In view of the naiveté of the "Human Brain Project" and the dichotomy of the concept of law, we can summarize that jurisprudence is not a closed system but is, like language, open. The formal rationality of decisions will at the latest encounter difficulties when the pressure of material rationality on the strict law reaches a level that necessitates

für Verwaltungsrecht, XVII (2018), p. 1264; Abel, note 16 above, pp. 304-307; Mario Martini and David Nink, "Wenn Maschinen entscheiden … Persönlichkeitsschutz in vollautomatisierten Verwaltungsverfahren", *Neue Zeitschrift für Verwaltungsrecht*, X (2017), pp. 681-682; Wischmeyer, note 6 above, pp. 61-65.

[19] See the references in Stephan Meder, "Leibniz und das autonome Fahren. Zur Vorgeschichte der Ideen von selbststeuernden Maschinen, technischer Kinetik und Robotik", in Bernd H. Oppermann and Jutta Stender-Vorwachs, *Autonomes Fahren. Rechtsprobleme, Rechtsfolgen, technische Grundlagen* (2d ed.; 2020), pp. 41–47.

adaptation to external events. Jurisprudence and academia tend to legitimize the need for adaptation by referring to the "circumstances of the individual case". It is true that it is mostly individual cases that reveal the inadequacy of formal rationality in decisions. This should not obscure the fact that the "circumstances of the individual case" reveal something very fundamental and general, namely that the law has an inherent situational openness to the uncertainty of the world.

Artificial intelligence has until now dealt "mainly with closed systems", as one expert put it recently.[20] The problems posed by open systems cannot be dealt with by computing power, even if it continues to increase exponentially in the coming years. It would be a feat necessitating the replication of human thought and decision-making processes as they are carried out in the human brain or consciousness. Nonetheless, the belief that the ability of human beings to think will one day be completely reproduceable by machines is widespread. However, the irrationality of current debates about artificial intelligence and the famous "visions of the future" should not be underestimated. Computer scientist Rodney Brooks boiled it down to a simple logical progression; from the "rise of more efficient internal combustion engines", many conclude that "warp drives" are now "within reach".[21] Critical voices attempt to

[20] Mühlenbein, note 12 above, p. 10.

[21] Rodney A. Brooks, "Die Verwechslung von Performanz und Kompetenz", in John Brockman, *Was sollen wir von künstlicher Intelligenz halten? Die führenden Wissenschaftler unserer Zeit über intelligente Maschinen* (2017), p. 152. The list of examples could easily be continued. For example, Raymond Kurzweil, a co-founder of algorithmic speech recognition, applies Moore's law of increasing computing power to the vision of mind uploading to end up with the prediction that, from 2025, it will be possible to produced copies of the human brain, and by 2045 at the latest, this natural-artificial intelligence would be ready to have conquer human mortality. See Michael Pilz, "Natürlich Unsterblich", *Die Welt*, 31 January 2020, p. 21. The noted computer pioneer and inventor of the Turing Test, Alan Turing (1912-1954), believed that chess and language could simply be treated as one and the same. However, whereas chess programs, as explained, can defeat most players today, there is no artificial system in sight that could even come close to speaking a language. See Mühlenbein, note 12 above, p. 10. For further examples of unbridled optimism and the irrationality of current debates, see Eberl, note 6 above, p. 9. The Covid-19 crisis appears to have further

repudiate the analogy between brain and computer with the claim that the open systems of thought and language will remain a human proprium for some considerable time.[22] This second age of the machine thus sheds new light on Savigny's famous comparison of law to language,[23] but no one can yet foresee what role algorithms will play in jurisprudence in the future. It is not beyond the bounds of possibility, for example, that they will one day determine legal judgments to such an extent that critics of formalism will once again step forward and call for the focus to return to the real world and everyday life. These critics should then refer to the dichotomy of the concept of law rather than to the irrationalism of a legal-philosophical monism.

fueled the visionaries' euphoria. "Our society will never be the same again". One lesson the virus could teach would be to "push us into the digital age with might and power". According to media theorist Peter Weibel, "Virus, Virality, Virtuality: Wie gerade die erste Ferngesellschaft der Menschheitsgeschichte entsteht", *Neue Zürcher Zeitung,* 20 March 2020 (available online). In opposition to this view, art theorist Bazon Brock offers some rather sarcastic remarks: The "flow of traffic becomes a flow of signs", the remains of "digestive processes are virtualized", because one only needs to "imagine" chewing and swallowing; this would indeed be an important step for the increase of the "power of abstraction" of evolution, namely to do without "life". Brock, "Das Leben nach dem Virus", *Die Welt,* 30 March 2020, p. 9 (available online). It may be recalled that life, abstraction, imagination, digestion, reality are keywords around which already Jhering's critique of the "judgment machine" revolves (see chapter 2).

[22] See the section on "Geist als Computer" in Siri Hustvedt, *Die Illusion der Gewissheit* (2018), pp. 193-203 [published in English as *The Delusions of Certainty*].

[23] Savigny, *Vom Beruf unsrer Zeit für Gesetzgebung und Rechtswissenschaft* (1814), p. 9.

Conclusion

"Law ex machina" is a dream that humankind has been dreaming for some time. The idea of a rule of law, a binding postulate, and uncompromised impartiality combined with the promise of for rationalization and simplification of the law must have made the mechanical application of law seem the ultimate goal in the first age of the legal machine. The term "subsumption machine" emerged only amid criticism of formalism and shared the same pejorative connotations as Jhering's "judgment machine" [Urteilsmaschine], Kantorowicz's "thinking machine" [Denkmaschine], or Max Weber's "paragraph automaton" [Paragraphenautomat] as devices into which "one throws the files at the top, together with costs and fees, so that it spits out the judgment at the bottom, along with the more or less valid reasons". All these machines were meant to caricature the kind of formalism where the judge can only repeat what the statues already provide. The target was a model that is still considered a "relic of the 19th century". Jhering and Kantorowicz in particular polemicized against what they saw already as a "subsumption-positivist jurisprudence" that believed that the person applying the law could find the correct outcome of the law "mechanically" and without any intervention on their part. This is to deliberately overlook the fact that early nineteenth century authors in particular, with their radical critique of codification and their interpretational doctrine based on tact, feeling and judgment, were the ones campaigning against any kind of automated or machine-like application of the law. Things are more complicated than often assumed, and anyone wanting to trace the narrative of automatic subsumption must be careful to distinguish between the different ages.

Discussions about legal machines hide methodological questions that have been answered differently at different times: Where is the seat of the law? From where does the law derive its validity? Where are the boundaries between law and not-law? First of all, two fundamental but opposing ideas can be identified which have remained in tension until today. The first of these is the distinction that must be made between rules imposed by an authority standing above society, and norms which grow independently of a sovereign will, as it were from within society. The two positions are based on differing ideas about the origin of laws; on the one hand rules imposed by authorities through statutes, on the other laws forming on their own, so to speak, as a "spontaneous order". Jurists usually illustrate this difference by dividing law into the written (*scriptum*) and the unwritten (*non scriptum*), with the *ius scriptum* expressing the will of a national legislator and the *ius non scriptum* expressing the forces of society. In this context, it is understood that within the framework of *ius non scriptum*, customary law and other sources of the law as well as jurisprudential law and judicial determination have a special role to play.

This first fundamental idea originated in the age of the Law of Reason, the so-called Codification Age, which produced the first major European legislative works in the form of the Preußisches Allgemeines Landrecht (1794), the French *Code Civil* (1804) and the Austrian Allgemeines Bürgerliches Gesetzbuch (1811). The fundamental idea still plays an important role on the European continent today, for example in legal education or in the teaching of methodology. Legal laypeople and popular philosophers also tend, as shown, to reduce law to its formal qualities. Likewise, the idea of codification seems to be experiencing an unexpected renaissance in the field of legal tech, which is a result of the fact that systems capable of learning depend on lawyers: Legal experts are called on to provide computer scientists, information technology specialists, and programmers with an idea of how legal reasoning works when they are attempting to transform jurisprudence into formal language. It is thus the responsibility of the legal experts to supply and maintain material suitable for feeding the systems. In their selection, they are guided by certain principles which, depending on their methodological preconceptions, are more oriented towards laws, dogmatics, or individual cases. One merely has to recall a study on the automated generation of law in which the authors declare the codification idea to be authoritative with the words: "Continental European law is based on the notion of positive written law and thus on a very strict separation between legislation and the application of law".[24]

After the turn of the nineteenth century, this view – which ultimately originated in the legal machine age – was subjected for the first time to a fundamental critique in the so-called codification controversy. Attention was drawn to the fact that there are other sources besides the written law that can also determine a legal decision. At this point the second fundamental idea enters the picture, that is to say, jurisprudential law, which is not based on the order of a sovereign will, but on the specific decision in an individual case. Practical application of the law generally resorts to it when legal rules are deficient or when they lead to unjust results.[25] Legislation and decisions in individual cases constitute the two poles that generate the difference between legal machines and judge-king.

It must be admitted that, from the perspective of legal streamlining, remarkable connections can also be found between statutory law and jurisprudential law. The similarity lies in the fact that jurisprudential law is also capable of abstraction and generating general concepts. Its generalizations or, in the words of Max Weber, "abstractions of the descriptive", in the form of "legal principles" still create problems in legal source theory for the continental European constitutional lawyer that are almost impossible to solve, as do dogmatics in general. Because jurisprudential law is not validated by the State, it must be legitimized in a particular way. In accordance with Max Weber and the teachings of the Historical School of Law, it could be said that jurisprudential law is usually customary law.[26] Thus, even the legal principles produced by jurists possess formal

[24] See the references in chapter 1.

[25] See Savigny's statements on the "method of Roman jurists" [Methode der Römischen Juristen], references to be found in Stephan Meder, *Mißverstehen und Verstehen. Savignys Grundlegung der juristischen Hermeneutik* (2004), pp. 72-74 (as well as chapter 7 at note 2). Weber's reflection on jurisprudence also essentially revolve around this kind of "method". See chapter 4.

[26] Max Weber, *Rechtssoziologie* (1922), in Weber, *Wirtschaft und Gesellschaft. Grundriß der verstehenden Soziologie*, ed. Johannes Winckelmann (5th ed.; 1985), p. 508.

qualities, provided that the *communis opinio* acknowledges them and that the legislative body does not contradict them. Customary law is therefore a supplement to statutory law and, as indicated earlier, may even overrule it in extreme cases.[27] Customary law may also be supplemented by additions by the judge and even be corrected under certain conditions. It relies on the same corrective mechanisms by which material elements are incorporated into statutory law in certain situations. The dual nature of the concept of law extends to all its sources.

Parallels exist not only between statutory and jurisprudential law, but also between jurisprudential and free law. Like the adherents of classical jurisprudential law, advocates of the doctrine of Free Law also assume that the law is created primarily from the decisions in individual cases. As Max Weber pointed out, the idea of jurisprudential law has now been extended by the doctrine of Free Law with its assertion that the "legal proposition" is merely "the secondary" and that the decision is the authoritative element. Accordingly, it is inaccurate to speak of a finding of law by "applying" general norms to a concrete set of facts, because the products of jurisprudence are "the actual location of 'applicable' law".[28] Such an approach would "always conclude from the individual to the individual" and never strive for "general propositions" in order to develop solutions based on them for future cases.

Just as the law in England, the doctrine of Free Law does not attempt to claim the application of general norms to the specific facts of the case.[29] Under these premises, the distance between (classical) jurisprudential law and the doctrine of Free Law is greater than that between jurisprudential law

[27] Weber, *Rechtssoziologie,* note 3 above, p. 508 (whose terminology is used here). This idea has been expressed by the authors of the BGB. Insofar as the legal solutions mentioned lie between the law and the individual case, it will be a matter of dogmatics. See in more detail Stephan Meder, "Was bedeutet Dogmatik? Eine Skizze aus rechtshistorischer Perspektive", in Andreas Raffeiner (ed.), *Auf der Klaviatur der Rechtsgeschichte - Festgabe für Kurt Ebert zum 75. Geburtstag* (2019), II, pp. 519-540.

[28] Weber, *Rechtssoziologie,* note 3 above, p. 507.

[29] Ibid., p. 457.

and statutory law. The common ground shared by properly understood statutory law – one that is not limited to its forms – and jurisprudential law is that both sources of law operate on the basis of a dual concept of law. In contrast, it is the declared goal of the doctrine of Free Law to dissolve all formal elements in favor of a teleological view. The doctrine of Free Law propagates a single-tier concept of law and is limited to the element that Max Weber characterized as the "material". Accordingly, the only law that would be valid that is law pronounced valid in a specific decision by judges. In contrast, (classical) jurisprudential law and statutory law can in principle predetermine rights by means of reliable forms. This is not changed by the fact that the right holders can be prevented from relying on them in specific cases.

So where does law reside when adaptive algorithms decide? In the law? In general legal principles? In decisions of individual cases? And how do the algorithms draw their conclusions? From the general to the particular? From the particular to the general? From the particular to the particular? As mentioned above, there are authors who believe that automata could decide based on a rule-based software written in accordance with the continental European model.[30] However, artificial intelligence now no longer works primarily with predefined rules, but on the basis of large amounts of data in the form of legal facts or case law, whereby the law is at best just one of many sources. Legal texts are transformed into mathematical equations on the basis of binary oppositions and analyzed according to their numerical frequency in relation to a specific legal issue. The systems look for correlations between given data points (variables) and develop assumptions and predictions about the plausibility of patterns using the tools of probability and statistics. The correlations determined in this way certainly have a certain general character, but autonomous systems do not articulate any general propositions which would be suitable for structuring a subject area, any more than dogmatics would be. They may be able to take into account evaluations or considerations, as far as these occur in earlier decisions and form any kind of pattern, but the subjects and

[30] See the references in chapter 1.

contents of these evaluations do not result from immediate contemplation or discursively actualized realities; instead, they derive from a comparison with patterns in past situations. Thus, in the end, it is not the individuality of specific persons affected or the singularity of the respective case that is the deciding factor, but the way in which the facts of the case in question relate to certain patterns or groups of patterns, as determined with the help of statistical procedures.

The general and the particular are one the pairs of concepts that have played a key role in philosophy and in many other disciplines since Antiquity, and, with its distinction between the general norm and the specific case, jurisprudence is no exception.[31] Autonomous systems lead to a fundamental dissolution of the categorical difference between the general and the specific. While it is true that algorithms can identify patterns of almost unlimited scale and at unmatchable speed, and can thus decide in an astonishing number of individual cases, they are unable to take into account circumstances that can justify a radical deviation from patterns in a specific situation, nor can they develop solutions that fall somewhere in between these patterns. In a way, they are blind in one eye, because they see only one side of the law – the side which is traditionally described by the term "form." As far as situational openness, the other side of law, is concerned, the systems, for all of their "intelligence," lack perception, feeling, physicality, tact, power of discernment, and indeed all of the elements that will continue to distinguish jurisprudence from any legal machine in the future.

[31] This is the subject of Meder, *Urteilen. Elemente von Kants reflektierender Urteilskraft in Savignys Lehre von der juristischen Entscheidungs- und Regelfindung* (1999).

Bibliography

"Urteil des Reichsgerichts vom 28. Januar 1905", *Entscheidungen des Reichsgerichts in Zivilsachen*, LX (1905), pp. 56-65.

Bundesgerichtshof, decision from 16 February 2005, *Neue Juristische Wochenschrift Rechtsprechungs-Report Zivilrecht*, IX (2005), pp. 619-621.

Bundesgerichtshof, decision from 12 July 2016, *Neue Juristische Wochenschrift*, XLVIII (2016), pp. 3512-3517.

Oberlandesgericht Stuttgart, decision from 7 February 2017, *Zeitschrift für Bank- und Kapitalmarktrecht*, V (2017), pp. 195-199.

Abel, Ralf B., "Automatisierte Entscheidungen im Einzelfall gem. Art. 22 DS-GVO", *Zeitschrift für Datenschutz*, VII (2018), pp. 304-307.

Adickes, Franz, *Zur Lehre von den Rechtsquellen: Insbesondere über die Vernunft und die Natur der Sache als Rechtsquellen und über das Gewohnheitsrecht* (1872), Kassel & Göttingen: Verlag von Georg H. Wigand.

Adrian, Axel, "Der Richterautomat ist möglich – Semantik ist nur eine Illusion", *Rechtstheorie*, XLVIII (2017), pp. 77-121.

Auer, Marietta, *Der privatrechtliche Diskurs der Moderne* (2014), Tübingen: Mohr Siebeck.

Bachelard, Gaston, "Der Mythos der Verdauung", in: id., *Die Bildung des wissenschaftlichen Geistes: Beitrag zu einer Psychoanalyse der objektiven Erkenntnis* (2nd ed.; 1978), pp. 251-268, Frankfurt a.M.: Suhrkamp.

Barros, Rhuan; Peres, André; Lorenzi, Fabiana; Krug Wives, Leandro and Etiene Hubert da Silva Jaccottet, "Case Law Analysis with Machine Learnig in Brazilian Court", in: Malek Mouhoub, Samira Sadaoui, Otmane Ait Mohamed and Moonis Ali (eds.), *Recent Trends and Future Technology in Applied Intelligence: 31st International Conference on Industrial Engineering and Other Applications of Applied Intelligent Systems, IEA/AIE 2018, Montreal, QC, Canada, June 25-28, 2018: proceedings* (2018), Cham: Springer, pp. 857-868.

Barth, Ulrike, "Legal Tech in Deutschland – zwischen Buzz Word und Anwaltsschreck", in: Markus Hartung, Micha-Manuel Bues and Gernot Halbleib (eds.), *Legal Tech. Die Digitalisierung des Rechtsmarktes* (2018), Munich: C.H.BECK/ Vahlen, pp.47-52.

Beck, Hans Ulrich and Harald Szeemann (eds.), *Die Junggesellenmaschine* (2nd ed.; 1999), Vienna, New York: Springer Verlag.

Behrends, Okko, *Struktur und Wert. Zum institutionellen und prinzipiellen Denken im geltenden Recht* (1990), in: id., *Institut und Prinzip: Siedlungsgeschichtliche Grundlagen, philosophische Einflüsse und das Fortwirken der beiden republikanischen Konzeptionen in den kaiserzeitlichen Rechtsschulen,* Vol. I (2004), Göttingen: Wallstein Verlag, pp. 55-89.

Behrends, Okko, "Nachruf Wieacker", *Zeitschrift der Savigny-Stiftung für Rechtsgeschichte (Romanistische Abteilung),* CXII (1995), pp. XIII-LXII.

Behrends, Okko, "Die rechtsethischen Grundlagen des Privatrechts", in: Franz Bydlinski and Theo Mayer-Maly (eds.), *Die ethischen Grundlagen des Privatrechts* (1994), Vienna: Verlag Österreich, pp. 1-33.

Beierle, Christoph and Gabriele Kern-Isberner, *Methoden wissensbasierter Systeme. Grundlagen, Algorithmen, Anwendungen* (6th ed.; 2019), Wiesbaden: Springer Vieweg.

Bentham, Jeremy, *Works, Part II* (1838), Edinburgh: William Tait.

Bentley, Arthur Fisher. *The Process of Government. A Study of Social Pressures* (1908), Chicago: University of Chicago Press, pp. 56-90.

Berger, Ariane, "Der automatisierte Verwaltungsakt", *Neue Zeitschrift für Verwaltungsrecht,* XVII (2018), pp. 1260-1264.

Beseler, Georg, *Volksrecht und Juristenrecht* (1843), Leipzig: Weidmann.

Bodin, Jean, *Sechs Bücher über den Staat* (1576), ed. Peter Cornelius Mayer-Tasch (1981), Munich: Beck.

Breuer, Stefan, *Anatomie der Konservativen Revolution* (2nd ed.; 1995), Darmstadt: Wissenschaftliche Buchgesellschaft (wbg).

Britz, Gabriele, *Einzelfallgerechtigkeit versus Generalisierung: verfassungsrechtliche Grenzen statistischer Diskriminierung* (2008), Tübingen: Mohr Siebeck.

Brock, Bazon, "Das Leben nach dem Virus", *Die Welt*, 30 March 2020, p. 9. Available online at: https://bazonbrock.de/werke/detail/die_welt-3831.html [last accessed 11 October 2022].

Brooks, Rodney A., "Die Verwechslung von Performanz und Kompetenz", in: John Brockman, *Was sollen wir von künstlicher Intelligenz halten? Die führenden Wissenschaftler unserer Zeit über intelligente Maschinen* (2017), Frankfurt a.M.: Fischer Taschenbuch, pp.149-152.

Büchel, Jochen, *Psychologie der Materie*: *Vorstellungen und Bildmuster von der Assimilation von Nahrung im 17. und 18. Jahrhundert unter besonderer Berücksichtigung des Paracelsismus* (2005), Würzburg: Königshausen & Neumann.

Bülow, Oskar, *Gesetz und Richteramt* (1885), Leipzig: Duncker & Humblot.

Busse, Dietrich, *Juristische Semantik. Grundfragen der juristischen Interpretationstheorie in sprachwissenschaftlicher Sicht* (1993), Berlin: Duncker & Humblot.

Busse, Dietrich, "Textlinguistik und Rechtswissenschaft", in: Klaus Brinker, Gerd Antos, Wolfgang Heinemann and Sven Frederik Sager (eds.), *Text- und Gesprächslinguistik, 1st half vol. Handbücher zur Sprach- und Kommunikationswissenschaft, Vol. XVI.I* (2000), Berlin, New York: De Gruyter, pp. 803-811.

Canaris, Claus-Wilhelm, "Wandlungen des Schuldvertragsrechts – Tendenzen zu seiner Materialisierung", *Archiv für die civilistische Praxis*, CC (2000), pp. 273-364.

Cardozo, Benjamin N., *The nature of the judicial process* (1921), New Haven: Yale University Press.

Casper, Gerhard, *Juristischer Realismus und politische Theorie im amerikanischen Rechtsdenken* (1967), Berlin: Duncker & Humblot.

Coing, Helmut and Gerhard Immel (eds.), *Hermann Kantorowicz - Rechtshistorische Schriften* (1970), Karlsruhe: C.F. Müller.

Cohen, Felix S., *THE LEGAL CONSCIENCE: Selected papers of Felix S. Cohen*, ed. Lucy Kramer Cohen, forew. Felix Frankfurter, introd. Eugene V. Rostow (1960), New Haven: Yale University Press.

Danaher, John, "The Threat of Algocracy: Reality, Resistance and Accomodation", *Philosophy & Technology*, XXIX (2016), pp. 245-268.

Descartes, René, "Beschreibung des menschlichen Körpers und aller seiner Funktionen, ebenso von denen, die nicht von der Seele abhängen, wie von denen, die von ihr abhängig sind, außerdem über die wesentliche Ursache für die Bildung seiner Glieder", in: id., Über den Menschen (1632) sowie Beschreibung des menschlichen Körpers (1648), ed. Karl Eduard Rothschuh (1969), Heidelberg: Schneider Verlag, pp. 137-194.

Dessauer, Friedrich, *Technische Kultur? Sechs Essays* (1908), Kempten, Munich: Verlag der Jos. Kösel'schen Buchhandlung.

Dilcher, Gerhard, "Von der Rechtsgeschichte zur Soziologie. Max Webers Auseinandersetzung mit der Historischen Rechtsschule" (2007), in: id. (ed.), *Die Germanisten und die Historische Rechtsschule: Bürgerliche Wissenschaft zwischen Romantik, Realismus und Rationalisierung* (2017), Frankfurt a.M.: Vittorio Klostermann, pp. 393-413.

Dilcher, Gerhard and Susanne Lepsius (eds.), *Max Weber-Gesamtausgabe, Abteilung I: Schriften und Reden, Vol. 1: Zur Geschichte der Handelsgesellschaften im Mittelalter: Schriften 1889 - 1894* (2008), Tübingen: Mohr.

Dreyfuß, Hubert L. and Stuart E. Dreyfuß, *Künstliche Intelligenz. Von den Grenzen der Denkmaschine und dem Wert der Intuition* (1987), Reinbek bei Hamburg: Rowohlt.

Eberl, Ulrich, "Was ist künstliche Intelligenz - was kann sie leisten?", *Aus Politik und Geschichte: Zeitschrift der Bundeszentrale für Politische Bildung*, LXVIII (2018), pp. 8-14.

Ehrlich, Eugen, "Die juristische Logik", *Archiv für die civilistische Praxis*, CXV (1917), (2nd ed.; 1918), pp. 125-439.

Engisch, Karl, *Logische Studien zur Gesetzesanwendung* (3rd ed.; 1963), Heidelberg: Winter.

Erbguth, Jörn, "Juristische Entscheidungen nach maschinellem Bauchgefühl", *Deutsche Richterzeitung*, 2018, pp. 130-131.Erichsen, Hans-Uwe and Dirk Ehlers (eds.), *Allgemeines Verwaltungsrecht* (14th ed.; 2010), Berlin: de Gruyter.

Ertel, Wolfgang, *Grundkurs Künstliche Intelligenz: eine praxisorientierte Einführung* (4th ed.; 2016), Wiesbaden: Springer Vieweg.

Eyth, Max "Poesie und Technik. Vortrag gehalten vor der Hauptversammlung des Vereins Deutscher Ingenieure zu Frankfurt am Main am 6. Juni 1904", in: id., *Lebendige Kräfte. Sieben Vorträge aus dem Gebiet der Technik* (1919), Berlin: Springer Verlag, pp. 1-22.

Falk, Ulrich, *Ein Gelehrter wie Windscheid. Erkundungen auf den Feldern der sogenannten Begriffsjurisprudenz* (1989), Frankfurt a.M.: Klostermann.

Fischer, Thomas, "'Terror' – Ferdinand von Schirach auf allen Kanälen", *ZEIT ONLINE*, 18 October 2016. Available at: https://www.zeit.de/gesellschaft/zeitgeschehen/2016-10/ard-fernsehen-terror-ferdinand-von-schirach-fischer-im-recht [last accessed 10 October 2022].

Flavius, Gnaeus, *Der Kampf um die Rechtswissenschaft* (1906), Heidelberg: Winter.

Foucault, Michel, *Raymond Roussel* (1989), Frankfurt a.M.: Suhrkamp.

Forsthoff, Ernst, "Hermeneutische Studien", in id.: *Recht und Sprache: Prolegomena zu einer richterlichen Hermeneutik* (1940), Halle an der Saale: Niemeyer, pp. 18-44.

Frank, Jerome, *Law and the Modern Mind* (1931), New York: Brentano.

Fries, Martin, *Legal Tech, lecture slides* (2018), Unit 3 'Künstliche juristische Intelligenz', p. 8. Available online at: https://www.jura.uni-münchen.de/personen/f/fries_engel__martin/veranstaltungen/vorlessung-legaltech/index.html [last accessed: 11 March 2020].

Fuchs, Ernst, *Juristischer Kulturkampf* (1912), Karlsruhe: Braun.

Fuchs, Ernst, *Jhering und die Freirechtsbewegung* (1918/19), in: id., *Gerechtigkeitswissenschaft: ausgewählte Schriften zur Freirechtslehre,* ed. Albert S. Foulkes (1965), Karlsruhe: Müller Verlag, pp. 181-191.

Fuchs, Ernst, *Begriffsjurisprudenz* (1912), in: *Gesammelte Schriften über Freirecht und Rechtsreform,* Vol. 2, ed. Albert S. Foulkes (1973), Aalen: Scientia-Verlag, pp.43-60.

Fuchs, Ernst, *Gefühlsjurisprudenz* (1912), in: *Gesammelte Schriften über Freirecht und Rechtsreform,* Vol. 2, ed. Albert S. Foulkes (1973), Aalen: Scientia-Verlag, pp.61-74.

Gadamer, Hans-Georg, *Wahrheit und Methode: Grundzüge einer philosophischen Hermeneutik* (1960), Tübingen: Mohr.

Gephart, Werner, *Gesellschaftstheorie und Recht - Das Recht im soziologischen Diskurs der Moderne* (1993), Frankfurt a.M.: Suhrkamp.

Gephart, Werner and Siegfried Hermes (eds.), *Max Weber-Gesamtausgabe, Abteilung I: Schriften und Reden, Vol. 22: Wirtschaft und Gesellschaft, Part 3: Recht* (2010), Tübingen: Mohr, pp. 274-639 (MWG I/22-3).

Gerathewohl, Peter, *Erschliessung unbestimmter Rechtsbegriffe mit Hilfe des Computers: ein Versuch am Beispiel der „angemessenen Wartezeit" bei § 142 StGB* (1987), Tübingen: Univ. Dissertation.

Gierke, Otto von, *Das deutsche Genossenschaftsrecht, Vol. II* (1873), Berlin: Weidmann.

Götz von Olenhusen, Albrecht, *Hintergründe zu Max Webers Presse-Enquete und das Presse- und Urheberrecht seiner Zeit* (2015), Bern: Stämpfli Verlag AG.

Graevenitz, Albrecht von, "'Zwei mal Zwei ist Grün' – Mensch und KI im Vergleich", *Zeitschrift für Rechtspolitik,* VIII (2018), p. 238-241.

Gräwe, Svenja Lena, *Die Entstehung der Rechtsinformatik. Wissenschaftsgeschichtliche und -theoretische Analyse einer Querschnittsdisziplin* (2011), Hamburg: Verlag Dr. Kovač.

Gruchmann, Lothar, *Justiz im Dritten Reich 1933-1940: Anpassung und Unterwerfung in der Ära Gürtner* (1988), Munich: Oldenbourg.

Gurvitch, Georges, *Grundzüge der Soziologie des Rechts* (2nd ed.; 1974), Darmstadt: Luchterhand.

Günzl, Clara, "Subsumtionsautomaten und -maschinen. Rechtshistorische Anmerkungen zu einem beliebten Vorwurf", *JuristenZeitung*, LXXIV (2019), pp. 180-188.

Haferkamp, Hans-Peter, "§ 242, Leistung nach Treu und Glauben", in: Mathias Schmoeckel, Joachim Rückert and Reinhard Zimmermann (eds.), *Historisch-kritischer Kommentar zum BGB Vol. II: Schuldrecht. Allgemeiner Teil. 1. Teilband: vor § 241 – § 304. 2. Teilband: §§ 305–432* (2007), Tübingen: Mohr Siebeck, pp. 274-364.

Haferkamp, Hans-Peter, "Lernen aus der Rechtsgeschichte? Hermann Kantorowicz und Friedrich Carl von Savigny", *JuristenZeitung*, LXXIV (2019), pp. 901-910.

Haferkamp, Hans-Peter, *Georg Friedrich Puchta und die "Begriffsjurisprudenz"* (2004), Frankfurt a.M.: Klostermann.

Hager, Günter, *Strukturen des Privatrechts in Europa: eine rechtsvergleichende Studie* (2012), Tübingen: Mohr Siebeck.

Harbou, Frederik v., "Abschied vom Einzelfall? - Perspektiven der Digitalisierung von Verwaltungsverfahren", *JuristenZeitung*, LXXV (2020), pp. 340-348.

Hartwieg, Oskar, *Tatsachen- und Normarbeit im Rechtsvergleich: ausgewählte Aufsätze* (2003), Tübingen: Mohr Siebeck.

Hastedt, Heiner, *Aufklärung und Technik. Grundprobleme einer Ethik der Technik* (1991), Frankfurt a.M.: Suhrkamp.

Hatschek, Julius, *Englisches Staatsrecht mit Berücksichtigung der für Schottland und Irland geltenden Sonderheiten, Vol. I: Die Verfassung* (1905), Tübingen: Mohr.

Hegel, Georg Friedrich Wilhelm, *Grundlinien der Philosophie des Rechts* (1821), Berlin: Nicolai.

Heindl, Robert, *Meine Reise nach den Strafkolonien* (1913), Berlin, Vienna: Ullstein.

Henkel, Thomas, *Begriffsjurisprudenz und Billigkeit. Zum Rechtsformalismus der Pandektistik nach G.F. Puchta* (2004), Cologne, Weimar, Vienna: Böhlau Verlag.

Hildebrandt, Heinz, *Rechtsfindung im neuen deutschen Staate. Ein Beitrag zur Rezeption und den Rechtsquellen, zur Auslegung und Ergänzung des Gesetzes* (1935), Berlin, Leipzig: Walter de Gruyter.

Hirsch, Philipp-Alexander, *Kants Einleitung in die Rechtslehre von 1784. Immanuel Kants Rechtsbegriff in der Moralvorlesung „Mrongovius II" und der Naturrechtsvorlesung „Feyerabend" von 1784 sowie in der „Metaphysik der Sitten" von 1797* (2012), Göttingen: Universitätsverlag.

Hobbes, Thomas, *Leviathan: Or the Matter, Forme and Power of a Commonwealth Ecclesiastical and Civil* (1651), ed. Michael Joseph Oakeshott (1957), Oxford: Blackwell.

Hobbes, Thomas, *Leviathan oder Stoff, Form und Gewalt eines bürgerlichen und kirchlichen Staates*, ed. Iring Fetscher (1966), Frankfurt a.M.: de Gruyter.

Höbenreich, Evelyn, *Marianne Webers "Ehefrau und Mutter in der Rechtsentwicklung". Beziehungsmodelle zwischen römischem Recht und deutscher Kodifizierung* (2018), Lecce: Edizioni Grifo.

Hoffmann-Riem, Wolfgang, "Verhaltenssteuerung durch Algorithmen", *Archiv des öffentlichen Rechts*, CXLII (2017), pp. 1-42.

Höffe, Otfried, "Einführung", in: id., *Immanuel Kant, Metaphysische Anfangsgründe der Rechtslehre* (1999), Berlin: Akademie Verlag, pp. 1-18.

Höffe, Otfried, "Der Kategorische Rechtsimperativ. 'Einleitung in die Rechtslehre'", in: id., *Immanuel Kant, Metaphysische Anfangsgründe der Rechtslehre* (1999), Berlin: Akademie Verlag, pp. 41-62.

Holloway, William, *System of the Modern Roman Law, Volume I* (1867), Madras: J. Higginbotham. Available online at: https://babel.hathitrust.org/cgi/pt?id=wu.89097651095&view=1up&seq=7&skin=2021 [last accessed 10 October 2022].

Holmes, Oliver Wendell, "Book Notices: A Selection of Cases on the Law of Contracts, with a Summary of the Topics covered by the Cases, by C. C. Langdell", *The American Law Review*, XIV (1880), pp. 233-235.

Horwitz, Morton J., "The Rise of Legal Formalism", *The American Journal of Legal History*, XIX (1975), pp. 251-264.

Hoyos, Roman J., "Beyond Classical Legal Thought: Law and Governance in Postbellum America", in: Sally E. Hadden and Alfred L. Brophy (eds.), *A companion to American legal history* (2013), Chichester: John Wiley & Sons, pp. 86-104.

Hugo, Gustav, "Rezension Schlosser Briefe über die Gesetzgebung überhaupt, und den Entwurf des Preussischen Gesetzbuchs insbesondere (1789)", in: *Beyträge zur civilistischen Bücher-Kenntniß der letzten vierzig Jahre: aus den Göttingischen Gelehrten Anzeigen und den Vorreden besonders zu den Theilen des civilistischen Cursus, zusammen abgedruckt und mit Zusätzen begleitet, Vol. I: 1788-1807* (1828), Berlin: Mylius, p. 114.

Hustvedt, Siri, *Die Illusion der Gewissheit* (2018), Reinbek: Rowohlt, pp. 193-203.

Jandach, Thomas, *Juristische Expertensysteme: Methodische Grundlagen ihrer Entwicklung* (1993), Berlin: Springer.

Jansen, Nils, "Der Gegenstand der Rechtswissenschaft", *JuristenZeitung*, LXXV (2020), pp. 213-223.

Jeand'Heur, Bernd, "Die neuere Fachsprache der juristischen Wissenschaft seit der Mitte des 19. Jahrhunderts unter besonderer Berücksichtigung von Verfassungsrecht und Rechtsmethodik", in: Hugo Steger and Herbert Ernst Wiegand (eds.), *Handbücher zur Sprach- und Kommunikationswissenschaft*, Vol. XIV.I (1998), Berlin: Verlag, pp. 1286-1295.

Jhering, Rudolf von, "Friedrich Karl von Savigny", *Jherings Jahrbücher für die Dogmatik des bürgerlichen Rechts,* 5 (1861), pp. 354-377.

Jhering, Rudolf von, *Gesammelte Aufsätze aus den Jahrbüchern für die Dogmatik des heutigen römischen und deutschen Privatrechts, Vol. 2: Abhandlungen aus dem 5. bis 15. Bande der Jahrbücher* (1882), Jena: Fischer.

Jhering, Rudolf von, *Der Zweck im Recht*: *Band I* (3rd ed.; 1893), Leipzig: Breitkopf & Härtel.

Jhering, Rudolf von, *Der Kampf ums Recht* (5th ed.; 1977), Frankfurt a.M.: Klostermann.

Jhering, Rudolf von, *Scherz und Ernst in der Jurisprudenz* (9th ed.; 1904), Leipzig: Breitkopf & Härtel.

Jhering, Rudolf von, "Wiener Antrittsvorlesung (1868)", in: Okko Behrends, *Ist die Jurisprudenz eine Wissenschaft?: Jherings Wiener Antrittsvorlesung vom 16. Oktober 1868* (1998), Göttingen: Wallstein-Verlag, pp. 19-92.

Jhering, Rudolf von, *Geist des römischen Rechts auf den verschiedenen Stufen seiner Entwicklung: Zweiter Theil, Erste Abtheilung* (4th ed.; 1880), Leipzig: Breitkopf & Härtel.

Jhering, Rudolf von, *Geist des römischen Rechts auf den verschiedenen Stufen seiner Entwicklung: Zweiter Theil, Zweite Abtheilung* (4th ed.; 1883), Leipzig: Breitkopf & Härtel.

Jhering, Rudolf von, *Geist des römischen Rechts auf den verschiedenen Stufen seiner Entwicklung, Dritter Theil, Erste Abtheilung* (4th ed.; 1888), Leipzig: Breitkopf & Härtel.

Jost, David and Johann Kempe, "E-Justice in Deutschland. Eine Bestandsaufnahme zur Digitalisierung der Justiz", *Neue Juristische Wochenschrift*, XXXVIII (2017), pp. 2705-2708.

Jung, Erich, *Das Problem des natürlichen Rechts* (1912), Leipzig: Duncker & Humblot.

Kafka, Franz, "In der Strafkolonie", in: id., *In der Strafkolonie. Ein Landarzt. Ein Hungerkünstler* (2011), Cologne: Anaconda Verlag.

Kafka, Franz, *In the Penal Colony / In der Strafkolonie: Bilingual Edition: English - German / Zweisprachige Ausgabe: Englisch – Deutsch* (2017), BookRix [eBook].

Kant, Immanuel, *Kritik der Urteilskraft: Text auf Grundlage der drei Originalausgaben von 1790, 1793 und 1799*, eds. Karl Vorländer and Heiner F. Klemme (7th ed.; 1990), Hamburg: Meiner.

Kant, Immanuel, *Kant's Critique of Judgment*, ed. John H. Bernard (1914), London: Macmillan.

Kant, Immanuel, *Kritik der reinen Vernunft* (2nd ed.; 1787), Riga: Hartknoch.

Kant, Immanuel, *Metaphysik der Sitten* (1797), *Werkausgabe, Vol. VIII*, ed. Wilhelm Weischedel (10th ed.; 1993), Frankfurt a.M.: Suhrkamp.

Kantorowicz, Hermann U., "Die Epochen der Rechtswissenschaft", *Die Tat*, VI (1914), pp. 345-361

Kantorowicz, Hermann U., *Rechtswissenschaft und Soziologie* (1911), in: id., *Rechtswissenschaft und Soziologie: ausgewählte Schriften zur Wissenschaftslehre,* ed. Thomas Würtenberger (1962), Karlsruhe: Müller, pp. 117-144.

Kantorowicz, Hermann U., "Was ist uns Savigny?", *Recht und Wirtschaft,* I (1912), pp. 47-54.

Kantorowicz, Hermann U., "Iherings Bekehrung", *Deutsche Richterzeitung,* VI (1914), pp. 84-87.

Kantorowicz, Hermann U., *Aus der Vorgeschichte der Freirechtslehre* (1925), in: id., *Rechtswissenschaft und Soziologie: Ausgewählte Schriften zur Wissenschaftslehre,* ed. Thomas Würtenberger (1962), Karlsruhe: Müller, pp.41-67.

Kennedy, Duncan, "Legal Formality", *The Journal of Legal Studies,* II (1973), pp. 351-398.

Kennedy, Duncan, "The disenchantment of logically formal legal rationality: Or, Max Weber's sociology in the genealogy of the contemporary mode of western legal thought", *Hastings Law Journal,* LV (2004), pp. 1031-1076.

Keppeler, Lutz Martin, *Oswald Spengler und die Jurisprudenz: die Spenglerrezeption in der Rechtswissenschaft zwischen 1918 und 1945, insbesondere innerhalb der "dynamischen Rechtslehre", der Rechtshistoriographie und der Staatsrechtswissenschaft* (2014), Tübingen: Mohr Siebeck.

Kierulff, Johann Friedrich, *Theorie des Gemeinen Civilrechts, Vol. I* (1839), Altona: Hammerich.

Kilian, Wolfgang, *Juristische Entscheidung und elektronische Datenverarbeitung. Methodenorientierte Vorstudie* (1974), Frankfurt a.M.: Athenäum-Verlag.

Kirchberger, Lida, *Franz Kafka's Use of Law in Fiction. A New Interpretation of In der Strafkolonie, Der Prozess, and Das Schloss* (1986), New York: Lang.

Kittler, Wolf, "In dubio pro reo. Kafkas 'Strafkolonie'", in: Arne Höcker and Oliver Simons (eds.), *Kafkas Institutionen* (2007), Bielefeld: transcript Verlag, pp. 56-68.

Klafki, Anika; Würkert, Felix; Winter, Tina; Ernst, Christian; Mattig, Daniel; Djeffal, Christian; Schaar, Peter and Theresa Witt (eds.), *Digitalisierung und Recht: Tagung des eingetragenen Vereins Junge Wissenschaft im Öffentlichen Recht an der Bucerius*

Law School am 26. November 2016 (2017), Hamburg: Bucerius Law School Press.

Kocourek, Albert, "Formal Relation Between Law and Discretion", *Illinois Law Review*, IX (1914), pp. 225-245.

Koschorke, Albrecht; Lüdemann, Susanne; Frank, Thomas and Ethel Matala de Mazza, *Der fiktive Staat: Konstruktionen des politischen Körpers in der Geschichte Europas* (2007), Frankfurt a.M: Fischer Taschenbuch Verlag.

Kotsoglou, Kyriakos N., "Subsumtionsautomat 2.0. Über die (Un-)Möglichkeit einer Algorithmisierung der Rechtserzeugung", *JuristenZeitung*, LXIX (2014), pp. 451-457.

Kramer, Alan, "Kriegsrecht und Kriegsverbrechen", in: Gerhard Hirschfeld, Gerd Krumreich and Irina Renz (eds.), *Enzyklopädie Erster Weltkrieg* (3rd ed.; 2009), Paderborn: Schöningh, pp. 281-292.

Kudlich, Hans, "Information als Herausforderung und Informatik als Hilfsmittel für die Rechtsanwendung im Straf- und Strafprozessrecht", in: Jürgen Taeger and Irini Vassilaki (eds.), *Rechtsinformatik und Informationsrecht im Spannungsfeld von Recht, Informatik und Ökonomie : 1. Wissenschaftliches Forum für Recht & Informatik* (2009), Edewecht: Oldenburger Verl. für Wirtschaft, Informatik und Recht, pp. 13-23.

Landau, Peter, "Die Rechtsquellenlehre in der deutschen Rechtswissenschaft des 19. Jahrhunderts", in: Claes Petersson (ed.), *Juristische Theoriebildung und rechtliche Einheit: Beiträge zu einem rechtshistorischen Seminar in Stockholm im September 1992* (1993), Lund: Inst. för Rättshistorisk Forskning, pp. 69-89.

Larenz, Karl, "Der Vertrag als Gestaltungsmittel der völkischen Ordnung", in: id., *Vertrag und Unrecht* (1937), Hamburg: Hanseatische Verlagsanstalt, pp. 31-36.

Leibniz, Gottfried Wilhelm, *Elementa Juris Naturalis* (1669-1671), in: id., *Sämtliche Schriften und Briefe. BAND 1: Sämtliche Schriften und Briefe (1663-1672)*, (2nd ed.; 1990), Berlin: Akademie Verlag, Akademie-Ausgabe VI 1.

Lossau, Norbert, "Diese Super-Software bringt sich übermenschliche Leistungen bei", *Welt*, 18 October 2017.

Available online at: https://www.welt.de/wissenschaft/article169782047 [last accessed 8 March 2020].

Lübbe-Wolff, Gertrud, *Das Dilemma des Rechts. Über Strenge, Milde und Fortschritt im Recht* (2017), Basel: Schwabe Verlag.

Lüke, Martina G., "'In the Penal Colony' and Beyond: Anxieties about Technology in an Era of Increasing Mechanization", *Journal of the Kafka Society of America*, XXXI-XXXII (2007-08), pp. 80-87.

Luhmann, Niklas, *Recht und Automation in der öffentlichen Verwaltung: eine verwaltungswissenschaftliche Untersuchung* (1966), Berlin: Duncker & Humblot.

Mäder, Claudia, "Der Philosophie steht eine neue grosse Zeit bevor", Interview with David Precht, *Neue Zürcher Zeitung*, 19 November 2016, p. 48.

Martini, Mario and David Nink, "Wenn Maschinen entscheiden … Persönlichkeitsschutz in vollautomatisierten Verwaltungsverfahren", *Neue Zeitschrift für Verwaltungsrecht*, X (2017), pp. 681-682.

Maschenbaur, Johannes Andreas Erdmann, "Des Herrn Vaucanson Schreiben an den Herrn Abt D.F.", in: id. (ed.), *Beschreibung eines mechanischen Kunst-Stucks und Avtomatischen Flöten-Spielers: so denen Herren von der Königlichen Academie der Wissenschaften zu Paris durch den Herrn Vaucanson Erfinder dieser Machine überreicht worden, samt Einer Description sowohl einer künstlich-gemachten Ente, die von sich selbst das Essen und Trincken hinein schluckt … und all dasjenige verrichtet/ was eine lebendige Ente thun kan; Als auch Einer andern gleichfalls wunderbaren Figur, welche mit der einen Hand die Trommel rühret, und mit der andern 20 unterschiedliche Arien auf einer Provence-Pfeiffe spielt und bläset; Nach dem Pariser-Exemplar übersetzt und gedruckt* (1748), Augsburg: Maschenbaur, pp. 21-24.

Matala de Mazza, Ethel, *Der verfaßte Körper: Zum Projekt einer organischen Gemeinschaft in der Politischen Romantik* (1999), Freiburg im Breisgau: Rombach.

Mecke, Christoph-Eric, *Begriff und System des Rechts bei Georg Friedrich Puchta* (2009), Göttingen: V&R unipress.

Mecke, Christoph-Eric, *Begriff des Rechts und Methode der Rechtswissenschaft bei Rudolf von Jhering* (2018), Göttingen: V&R unipress.

Meder, Stephan, "Franz Wieackers 'Wandlungen im Bilde der historischen Rechtsschule' neu gelesen: Ein schiefes Bild der Rechtsgeschichte?", in: *Festschrift für Albert Janssen* (forthcoming).

Meder, Stephan, *Schuld, Zufall, Risiko: Untersuchungen struktureller Probleme privatrechtlicher Zurechnung* (1993), Frankfurt a.M.: Klostermann.

Meder, Stephan, *Urteilen: Elemente von Kants reflektierender Urteilskraft in Savignys Lehre von der juristischen Entscheidungs- und Regelfindung* (1999), Frankfurt a.M.: Klostermann.

Meder, Stephan, *Mißverstehen und Verstehen. Savignys Grundlegung der juristischen Hermeneutik* (2004), Tübingen: Mohr Siebeck.

Meder, Stephan, *Ius non scriptum: Traditionen privater Rechtsetzung* (2nd ed.; 2009), Tübingen: Mohr Siebeck.

Meder, Stephan, *Doppelte Körper im Recht: Traditionen des Pluralismus zwischen staatlicher Einheit und transnationaler Vielheit* (2015), Tübingen: Mohr Siebeck.

Meder, Stephan, *Rechtsgeschichte: eine Einführung* (6th ed.; 2017), Cologne: Böhlau Verlag.

Meder, Stephan, *Der unbekannte Leibniz: Die Entdeckung von Recht und Politik durch Philosophie* (2018), Vienna, Cologne, Weimar: Böhlau Verlag.

Meder, Stephan, "Das Verbraucherwiderrufsrecht", *juris PraxisReport Bank- und Kapitalmarktrecht*, VII (2018).

Meder, Stephan, "Rudolf von Jhering und der Aufstand gegen den rechtswissenschaftlichen Formalismus", *JuristenZeitung*, LXXIV (2019), pp. 689-696.

Meder, Stephan, "Was bedeutet Dogmatik? Eine Skizze aus rechtshistorischer Perspektive", in: Andreas Raffeiner (ed.), *Auf der Klaviatur der Rechtsgeschichte - Festgabe für Kurt Ebert zum 75. Geburtstag*, Vol II (2019), Hamburg: Verlag Dr. Kovač, pp. 519-540.

Meder, Stephan, "Zwischen strengem Formalismus und totaler Materialisierung", *Kritische Justiz,* LII (2019), pp. 528-542.

Meder, Stephan, "Leibniz und das autonome Fahren. Zur Vorgeschichte der Ideen von selbststeuernden Maschinen, technischer Kinetik und Robotik", in: Bernd H. Oppermann and Jutta Stender-Vorwachs, *Autonomes Fahren. Rechtsprobleme, Rechtsfolgen, technische Grundlagen* (2nd ed.; 2020), Munich: C.H.Beck, pp. 41–47.

Meder, Stephan, "*Aequitas* und *ius strictum* in der Historischen Rechtsschule und Pandektistik", in: Matthias Armgardt and Hubertus Busche (eds.), *Recht und Billigkeit: zur Geschichte der Beurteilung ihres Verhältnisses* (2021), Tübingen: Mohr Siebeck, pp. 509-532.

Mihály, Csilla, "Franz Kafka: In der Strafkolonie", in: Zoltán Szendi (ed.), *Wechselwirkungen I: deutschsprachige Literatur und Kultur im regionalen und internationalen Kontext; Beiträge der internationalen Konferenz des Germanistischen Instituts der Universität Pécs vom 9. bis 11. September 2010* (2012), Vienna: Praesens Verlag, pp. 371-388.

Mommsen, Theodor, "Die Aufgabe der historischen Wissenschaft und die Bedeutung des römischen Rechts", in: id., *Gesammelte Schriften, Vol. III: Juristische Schriften* (1907), Berlin: Weidmann, pp. 580-600.

Mommsen, Wolfgang J. and Rita Aldenhoff (eds.), *Max Weber-Gesamtausgabe, Abteilung I, Vol. 4: Landarbeiterfrage, Nationalstaat und Volkswirtschaftspolitik. Schriften und Reden 1892-1899, 1st half-vol.* (1993), Tübingen: Mohr, pp. 526-534 (MWG I/4-1).

Mühlenbein, Heinz, "Grenzen der künstlichen Intelligenz - Ein Plädoyer für Bescheidenheit", *Künstliche Intelligenz,* IX (1995), pp. 1-14.

Müller, Hans-Peter, *Max Weber: eine Einführung in sein Werk* (2007), Cologne: Böhlau Verlag.

Müller-Erzbach, Rudolf, *Die Hinwendung der Rechtswissenschaft zum Leben und was sie hemmt* (1939), Tübingen: Mohr.

Müller-Seidel, Walter, *Die Deportation des Menschen. Kafkas Erzählung "In der Strafkolonie" im europäischen Kontext* (1986), Stuttgart: Metzler.

Mugdan, Benno (ed.), *Die gesammten Materialien zum Bürgerlichen Gesetzbuch für das Deutsche Reich: 5 Bände und Sachregister sowie Ergänzungsband, Vol. I: Einführungsgesetze und Allgemeiner Teil* (reprint; 1979), Aalen: Scientia Verlag.

Nipperdey, Hans Carl and Ludwig Enneccerus, *Allgemeiner Teil des Bürgerlichen Rechts* (15th ed.; 1960), Tübingen: Mohr.

Ofner, Julius, *Studien sozialer Jurisprudenz* (1894), Vienna: Hölder.

Ogorek, Regina, *Richterkönig oder Subsumtionsautomat? Zur Justiztheorie im 19. Jahrhundert* (1986), Frankfurt a.M.: Klostermann.

Oestmann, Peter, "Die Zwillingsschwester der Freiheit. Die Form im Recht als Problem der Rechtsgeschichte", in: id. (ed.), *Zwischen Formstrenge und Billigkeit: Forschungen zum vormodernen Zivilprozeß* (2009), Cologne: Böhlau Verlag, pp. 20–23.

Oexle, Otto Gerhard, "„Wirklichkeit" - „Krise der Wirklichkeit" - „Neue Wirklichkeit". Deutungsmuster und Paradigmenkämpfe in der deutschen Wissenschaft vor und nach 1933", in: Frank-Rutger Hausmann (ed.), *Die Rolle der Geisteswissenschaften im Dritten Reich 1933-1945* (2002), Munich: Oldenbourg, pp. 1-20.

Otto, Philipp in H. Radke, "Digitale Justiz aus dem Blickwinkel des Zukunftsforschers: Interview mit Philipp Otto", *Juris – Die Monatszeitschrift*, XII (2019), pp. 482–483.

Palandt, Otto, *Bürgerliches Gesetzbuch: BGB* (64th ed.; 2005), Munich: C.H. Beck.

Patel, Brijain R. and Kushik K. Rana, "A Survey on Decision Tree Algorithm. For Classification", *International Journal of Engineering Development and Research*, II (2014), pp. 1-5.

Pilz, Michael, "Natürlich Unsterblich", *Die Welt*, 31 January 2020, p. 21.

Polaschegg, Andrea, "Maschinen (nicht) verstehen. Das kollabierte Paradox in Franz Kafkas Erzählung In der Strafkolonie", *Deutsche Vierteljahrsschrift für*

Literaturwissenschaft und Geistesgeschichte, LXXXII (2008), pp. 654-679.

Pound, Roscoe, "Mechanical jurisprudence", *Columbia Law Review*, VIII (1908), pp. 605-623.

Pound, Roscoe, *The Spirit of the Common Law* (1921), Boston: Marshall Jones.

Priebe, Carsten and Vito von Eichborn, *Eine Reise durch die Aufklärung: Maschinen, Manufakturen und Mätressen; die Abenteuer von Vaucansons Ente oder die Suche nach künstlichem Leben* (2007), Norderstedt: Books on Demand.

Pringsheim, Fritz, *Beryt und Bologna* (1921), in: id., *Gesammelte Abhandlungen, Vol. I* (1961), Heidelberg: Winter, pp. 391-449.

Pringsheim, Fritz, *Höhe und Ende der römischen Jurisprudenz* (1933), in: id., *Gesammelte Abhandlungen, Vol. I* (1961), Heidelberg: Winter, pp. 391-449.

Pringsheim, Fritz, *Die archaistische Tendenz Justinians* (1929), in: id., *Gesammelte Abhandlungen, Vol. II* (1961), Heidelberg: Winter, pp. 9-40.

Puchta, Georg Friedrich, *Vorlesungen über das heutige römische Recht. Aus dessen Nachlaß*, ed. Adolf August Friedrich Rudorff, Vol. I (1847), Leipzig: Tauchnitz.

Queudot, Marc and Marie-Jean Meurs, "Artificial Intelligence and Predictive Justice: Limitations and Perspectives", in: Malek Mouhoub, Samira Sadaoui, Otmane Ait Mohamed and Moonis Ali (eds.), *Recent Trends and Future Technology in Applied Intelligence: 31st International Conference on Industrial Engineering and Other Applications of Applied Intelligent Systems, IEA/AIE 2018, Montreal, QC, Canada, June 25-28, 2018: proceedings* (2018), Cham: Springer, pp. 889-897.

Raabe, Oliver; Wacker, Richard; Oberle, Daniel; Baumann, Christian and Christian Funk, *Recht ex machina. Formalisierung des Rechts im Internet der Dienste* (2012), Berlin, Heidelberg: Springer-Verlag.

Rabban, David M., *Law's history: American legal thought and the transatlantic turn to history* (2013), Cambridge: Cambridge University Press.

Rathenau, Walther, *Zur Kritik der Zeit* (1912), Berlin: Fischer.

Rathenau, Walther, *Zur Mechanik des Geistes* (1913), Berlin: Fischer.

Rave, Dieter; Brinckmann, Hans and Klaus Grimmer (eds.), *Paraphrasen juristischer Texte. Referate und Protokolle der Arbeitstagung [der] Interdisziplinären Arbeitsgruppe "Analyse der juristischen Sprache" im Deutschen Rechenzentrum Darmstadt, 24.-26. Juni 1971* (1971), Darmstadt: Interdisziplinäre Arbeitsgruppe Analyse d. Jurist. Sprache.

Reimann, Mathias W., "Holmes' Common Law and German Legal Science", in: Robert W. Gordon (ed.), *The legacy of Oliver Wendell Holmes, Jr.* (1992), Stanford, Calif.: Stanford University Press., pp. 72-114.

Riskin, Jessica, "The Defecating Duck, or, the Ambiguous Origins of Artificial Life", *Critical Inquiry,* XXIX (2003), pp. 599-633.

Rivier, Alphonse, "Rudolf Von Jhering and Bernhard Windscheid", *The Juridical Review,* V (1893), pp. 1–12.

Roos, Nico, "Antiformale Tendenzen im modernen Recht – eine These Max Webers, diskutiert am Beispiel der Laienfrage", in: Stefan Breuer and Hubert Treiber (eds.), *Zur Rechtssoziologie Max Webers: Interpretation, Kritik, Weiterentwicklung* (1984), Opladen: Westdt. Verlag, pp. 223-267.

Röllicke, Hermann-Josef, "Wie kommt das Recht ins Gesetz? Kafkas Maschine in der Erzählung 'In der Strafkolonie'", *Coincidentia,* V (2014), pp. 343-374.

Savigny, Friedrich Carl von, *Vom Beruf unsrer Zeit für Gesetzgebung und Rechtswissenschaft* (1814), Heidelberg: Mohr & Zimmer.

Savigny, Friedrich Carl von, *System des heutigen römischen Rechts, Vol. I* (1840), Berlin: Veit.

Savigny, Friedrich Carl von, "Einleitung zu den Pandekten 1821/1822-1823/1824", in: Aldo Mazzacane (ed.), *Friedrich Carl von Savigny: Vorlesungen über juristische Methodologie 1802-1842* (2nd ed.; 2004), Frankfurt a.M.: Klostermann, pp. 271-275.

Savigny, Friedrich Carl von, "Einleitung zu den Pandekten 1827/1828-1841/1842", in: Aldo Mazzacane (ed.), *Friedrich*

Carl von Savigny: Vorlesungen über juristische Methodologie 1802-1842 (2nd ed.; 2004), Frankfurt a.M.: Klostermann, pp. 282-289.

Schapp, Jan, *Methodenlehre des Zivilrechts* (1998), Tübingen: J.C.B. Mohr.

Schild, Wolfgang, *Verwirrende Rechtsbelehrung: Zu Ferdinand von Schierachs 'Terror'* (2016), Münster: LIT Verlag.

Schmidt, Bruno, *Das Gewohnheitsrecht als Form des Gemeinwillens* (1899), Leipzig: Duncker & Humblot.

Schmidt, Katharina Isabel, "Der 'Formalismus-Mythos' im deutschen und amerikanischen Rechtsdenken des frühen 20. Jahrhunderts", *Der Staat,* LIII (2014), pp. 445–473.

Schott, Clausdieter, "Aequitas cerebrina", in: *Rechtshistorische Studien. Hans Thieme zum 70. Geburtstag zugeeignet von seinen Schülern,* ed. Bernhard Diestelkamp (1977), Cologne, Vienna: Boehlau, pp. 132-160.

Siebert, Wolfgang, *Verwirkung und Unzulässigkeit der Rechtsausübung: ein rechtsvergleichender Beitrag zur Lehre von den Schranken der privaten Rechte und zur exceptio doli (§§ 226, 242, 826 BGB): unter besonderer Berücksichtigung des gewerblichen Rechtsschutzes (§1 UWG)* (1934), Marburg: Elwert.

Siebert, Wolfgang, "Die neueste grundsätzliche Entscheidung des Reichsgerichts über die Verwirkung", *Juristische Wochenschrift,* 1937, pp. 2495 -2496.

Spengler, Oswald, *Der Untergang des Abendlandes: Umrisse einer Morphologie der Weltgeschichte* (1917), Beck'sche Sonderausgabe (1981), Munich: Beck.

Stalder, Felix, *Kultur der Digitalität* (2nd ed.; 2017), Berlin: Suhrkamp.

Steffen, Tilman, "Regierung will massenhafte Warenvernichtung stoppen", *Die Zeit,* 12 February 2020, p. 12.

Stollberg-Rilinger, Barbara, *Der Staat als Maschine: Zur politischen Metaphorik des absoluten Fürstenstaats* (1986), Berlin: Duncker & Humblot.

Susskind, Richard, *The End of Lawyers? Rethinking the Nature of Legal Services* (rev. ed.; 2010), Oxford: Oxford University Press.

Swedberg, Richard, *Max Weber and the Idea of Economic Sociology* (1998), Princeton, NJ.: Princeton University Press.

Tamanaha, Brian Z., *Beyond the formalist-realist divide: The role of politics in judging* (2010), Princeton, NJ.: Princeton University Press.

Tamanaha, Brian Z., *A Realistic Theory of Law* (2017), Cambridge: Cambridge University Press.

Treiber, Hubert, *Max Webers Rechtssoziologie - eine Einladung zur Lektüre* (2017), Wiesbaden: Harrassowitz Verlag.

Trubek, David M., "Max Weber on Law and the Rise of Capitalism", *Wisconsin Law Review*, III (1972), pp. 720-753.

Überegger, Oswald, "'Verbrannte Erde' und 'baumelnde Gehenkte'. Zur europäischen Dimension militärischer Normübertretungen im Ersten Weltkrieg", in: Sönke Neitzel and Daniel Hohrath (eds.), *Kriegsgreuel: Die Entgrenzung der Gewalt in kriegerischen Konflikten vom Mittelalter bis ins 20. Jahrhundert* (2008), Paderborn: Schöningh, pp. 241-278.

Unger, Sebastian, "Demokratische Herrschaft und künstliche Intelligenz", in: id. and Antje von Ungern-Sternberg (eds.), *Demokratie und künstliche Intelligenz* (2019), Tübingen: Mohr Siebeck, pp. 113-128.

Vogel, Friedemann, "Rechtslinguistik: Bestimmung einer Fachrichtung", in: Ekkehard Felder and Friedemann Vogel (eds.), *Handbuch Sprache im Recht* (2017), Berlin: De Gruyter, pp. 209-230.

Vuckovic, Vladan and Djordje Vidanovic, *A New Approach to Draw Detection by Move Repetition in Computer Chess Programming* (2014), Ort: Verlag. Available online at: https://arxiv.org/abs/cs/0406038 [last accessed 10 October 2022].

Wagenbach, Klaus (ed.), *Franz Kafka: In der Strafkolonie. Eine Geschichte aus dem Jahre 1914* (1998), Berlin: Wagenbach.

Wagner, Benno, "Connecting Cultures. Heinrich Rauchberg, Franz Kafka, and the Hollerith Machine", *Austriaca: Cahiers universitaires d'information sur l'Autriche*, LX (2005), pp. 53-68.

Wagner, Gerhard, "Materialisierung des Schuldrechts unter dem Einfluss von Verfassungsrecht und Europarecht", in: Uwe Blaurock and Günter Hager (eds.), *Obligationenrecht im 21. Jahrhundert* (2010), Baden-Baden: Nomos, pp. 13-84.

Wagner, Jens, "Legal Tech und Legal Robots in Unternehmen und den diese beratenden Kanzleien", *Betriebs-Berater*, XVII (2017), pp. 898-905.

Weber, Alfred, "Der Beamte", *Die neue Rundschau*, XXI (1910), pp. 1321-1339.

Weber, Max, "Politische Gemeinschaften", in: id., *Wirtschaft und Gesellschaft: Grundriß der verstehenden Soziologie*, ed. Johannes Winkelmann (5th ed.; 1985), Tübingen: Mohr, pp. 514-868, Tübingen.

Weber, Max "Soziologie der Herrschaft", in: id., *Wirtschaft und Gesellschaft. Grundriß der verstehenden Soziologie*, ed. Johannes Winckelmann (5th ed.; 1985), Tübingen: Mohr, pp. 541-868.

Weber, Max, *Die Geschichte der Handelsgesellschaften im Mittelalter. Nach südeuropäischen Quellen* (1889), Stuttgart: Enke.

Weber, Max, *Die römische Agrargeschichte in ihrer Bedeutung für das Staats- und Privatrecht* (1891), Stuttgart: Enke.

Weber, Max, *Wissenschaft als Beruf* (1919), in: *Gesammelte Aufsätze zur Wissenschaftslehre* (7th ed.; 1988), Tübingen: Mohr, pp. 582-613.

Weber, Max, "'Römisches' und 'deutsches' Recht" (1895), *Christliche Welt*, IX (1895), Sp. 521-525.

Weber, Max, "Besprechung von Philipp Lotmars 'Der Arbeitsvertrag, Bd. I'", *Archiv für Soziale Gesetzgebung und Statistik*, XVII (1902), pp. 723-734.

Weber, Max, "Brief an Professor Frensdorff in Göttingen v. 22. Januar 1887", in: id., *Jugendbriefe* (1936), Tübingen: Mohr, pp. 214-216.

Weber, Max, *Parlament und Regierung im neugeordneten Deutschland. Zur politischen Kritik des Beamtentums und Parteiwesens* (1918), in: id., *Gesammelte Politische Schriften*, ed. Johannes Winkelmann (2nd ed.; 1958), Tübingen: Mohr, pp. 306-443.

Weber, Max, *Rechtssoziologie* (1922), in: id., *Wirtschaft und Gesellschaft. Grundriß der verstehenden Soziologie*, ed. Johannes Winckelmann (5th ed.; 1985), Tübingen: Mohr, pp. 387-513.

Weber, Max, "Die Wirtschaft und die gesellschaftlichen Ordnungen", in: id., *Wirtschaft und Gesellschaft. Grundriß der verstehenden Soziologie*, ed. Johannes Winckelmann (5th ed.; 1985), Tübingen: Mohr, pp. 181-198.

Weber, Max, "Brief an Hermann Beck v. 12. September 1910", in: *Max Weber-Gesamtausgabe*, Abteilung II: Briefe, Vol. 6: Briefe 1909-1910 (1994), Tübingen: Mohr, pp. 606-607 (MWG II/6).

Weber, Max, *Economy and society. An outline of interpretive sociology*, eds. Guenther Roth and Claus Wittich (reprint.; 2007), Berkeley: University of California Press.

Weibel, Peter, "Virus, Virality, Virtuality: Wie gerade die erste Ferngesellschaft der Menschheitsgeschichte entsteht", *Neue Zürcher Zeitung*, 20 March 2020. Available online at: https://www.nzz.ch/feuilleton/virus-viralitaet-virtualitaet-peter-weibel-ueber-die-erste-ferngesellschaft-in-der-menschheitsgeschichte-ld.1547579 [last accessed 11 October 2022].

Weihermüller, Manfred, "Künftiges Informationsmanagement von Juristen", in: Carl-Eugen Eberle (ed.), *Informationstechnik in der Juristenausbildung: Ausbildungskonzepte, juristische PC-Pools, Nutzung von Datenbanken, Lernprogramme, Expertensysteme, Perspektiven, staatliche Förderung* (1989), Munich: Beck, pp. 192-204.

Weitin, Thomas, *Notwendige Gewalt. Die Moderne Ernst Jüngers und Heiner Müllers* (2003), Freiburg im Breisgau: Rombach.

Weitin, Thomas, "Revolution und Routine. Die Verfahrensdarstellung in Kafkas Strafkolonie", in: Arne Höcker and Oliver Simons (eds.), *Kafkas Institutionen* (2007), Bielefeld: Transcript, pp. 255-267.

Weizenbaum, Jospeh, *Die Macht der Computer und die Ohnmacht der Vernunft* (1977), Frankfurt a.M.: Suhrkamp.

White, Morthon G., *Social Thought in America: The Revolt Against Formalism* (1949), New York: Viking Press.

Wieacker, Franz, "Der Stand der Rechtserneuerung auf dem Gebiet des bürgerlichen Rechts", in: Karl August Eckhardt (ed.), *Deutsche Rechtswissenschaft: Im Auftrage der Reichsminister Bernhard Rust und Dr. Hans Frank* (1937), Hamburg: Hanseatische Verlagsanstalt, pp. 3-27.

Wieacker, Franz, "Richtermacht und privates Rechtsverhältnis. Eine Übersicht zum Stand der Problematik im Privatrecht", *Archiv des öffentlichen Rechts*, LXVIII (1938), pp. 1-39.

Wieacker, Franz, *Privatrechtsgeschichte der Neuzeit: Unter besonderer Berücksichtigung der deutschen Entwicklung* (2nd ed.; 1967), Göttingen: Vandenhoeck & Ruprecht.

Wieacker, Franz, "Recht und Automation", in: *Festschrift für Eduard Bötticher zum 70. Geburtstag am 29. Dezember 1969*, ed. Karl August Bettermann (1969), Berlin: Duncker & Humblot, pp. 383-404.

Wieacker, Franz, *Das Sozialmodell der klassischen Privatrechtsgesetzbücher und die Entwicklung der modernen Gesellschaft* (1953), in: id., *Industriegesellschaft und Privatrechtsordnung* (1974), Frankfurt a.M.: Athenäum-Fischer-Taschenbuch-Verlag, pp. 9-35.

Wieacker, Franz, "‚Wandlungen der Eigentumsverfassung' revisited", *Quaderni Fiorentini 5–6: Itinerari moderni della proprietá*, Tomo II (1976–77), pp. 841–843.

Wieacker, Franz, "Rechtsgewinnung durch elektronische Datenverarbeitung?", in: *Festschrift für Ernst von Caemmerer: zum 70. Geburtstag*, ed. Hans Claudius Ficker (1978), Tübingen: Mohr, pp. 45-71.

Wieacker, Franz, *A history of private law in Europe: With particular reference to Germany* (1995), Oxford: Clarendon Press.

Windscheid, *Die Voraussetzung* (1892), in: id., *Gesammelte Reden und Abhandlungen*, ed. Paul Oertmann (1904), Leipzig: Duncker & Humblot, pp. 375-409.

Winkler, Viktor, *Der Kampf gegen die Rechtswissenschaft: Franz Wieackers "Privatrechtsgeschichte der Neuzeit" und die deutsche Rechtswissenschaft des 20. Jahrhunderts* (2014), Hamburg: Verlag Dr. Kovač.

Wischmeyer, Thomas, "Regulierung intelligenter Systeme", *Archiv des öffentlichen Rechts*, CXLIII (2018), pp. 9-18.

Wolf, Christian, "Der Schlüssel zu einem effizienten Zivilprozessrecht", *Zeitschrift für Rechtspolitik*, VI (2018), pp. 183-185.

Wolffsteiner, Andreas, "'... a new human being, half robot and half four dimensional'. Duchamp, Roussel, Maschine", in: Helmar Schramm, Ludger Schwarte and Jan Lazardzig (eds.), *Spuren der Avantgarde: Theatrum machinarum, frühe Neuzeit und Moderne im Kulturvergleich* (2008), Berlin, New York: de Gruyter, pp. 391-406.

Wurzel, Karl Georg, *Das juristische Denken: Studie* (1904), Vienna: Perles.

Zweigert, Konrad, "Zum richterlichen Charisma in einer ethisierten Rechtsordnung", in: *Festgabe für Carlo Schmid zum 65. Geburtstag: Dargebracht von Freunden Schülern und Kollegen*, ed. Theodor Eschenburg (1962), Tübingen: Mohr, pp. 299-311.

Index of Names

The umlaut is disregarded in alphabetizing the entries below.

The Author

Stephan Meder is Professor of Civil Law and the History of Law at Leibniz Universität Hannover, where he has been a faculty member since 1998. His research interests lie in the areas of History and Philosophy of Law, much of his published work focusing on research of the eighteenth and nineteenth centuries.

www.ingramcontent.com/pod-product-compliance
Lightning Source LLC
LaVergne TN
LVHW092117300926
849161LV00002B/159